THANKSVEGAN:

A Vegan Cookbook For The Harvest Holiday

<<<<<<<<<<<<<>>>>>>>>>>>>>

Roberta Kalechofsky
&
Roberta Schiff

<<<<<<<<<<>>>>>>>>>>

Micah Publications, Inc.

Thanksvegan: A Vegan Cookbook For The Harvest Holiday, Copyright (c) 2012, Micah Publications, Inc.

Printed in the United States of America.
978-0-916288-59-4

About The Cover by Sara Feldman

The front cover is a detail from Sara Feldman's acrylic painting, Bounty. The original painting is 24" X 48" wide, and is from her Farmer's Market series. The back drawing is an original colored pencil-and-ink done for Thanksvegan.

Sara Feldman has a BFA from Carnegie Mellon University. She has been a member of the Depot Square Gallery of Lexington, MA for 28 years. She was a member of the Associated Artists of Pittsburgh and is a member of the Newton Art Association.

She has worked extensively in oil, acrylic, pen-and-ink and pencil. The majority of her oils and acrylics are landscapes, often inspired by the mountains where she has hiked and skied. Still life studies dominate her colored pencil, and pen-and-ink work.

She won the design competition for a large stained glass window for "The Sacred Space" at Northeastern University. She was an invited artist in two shows honoring Samuel Rosenberg, one at the Westmorland Museum of Art and one at the JCC of Pittsburgh. She was the illustrator for several years, and then publisher of a prize winning publication on the Holocaust. One of her paintings shown at the Carnegie Museum in Pittsburgh was selected for a purchase prize by the Latrobe School System.

She has done nine covers for Micah Publications, including, The Jewish Vegetarian Year Cookbook, 1997, Vegetarian Judaism, 1998, A Boy, a Chicken & the Lion of Judah, 2nd edition, 2011, and Thanksvegan, 2012.

MICAHBOOKS.COM

Dedicated to Jay Dinsha, 1933-2,000
Who founded the American Vegan Society
&
To his wife, Freya Smith Dinsha
Who Continues to Lead the Society

TABLE OF CONTENTS

~ INTRODUCTION ~

Jeremy Rifkin's fascinating book, *Beyond Beef: The Rise and Fall of the Cattle Culture,* appeared in 1992. It traced the symbolic significance of the cow and bull from their early appearance in the Indo-European Kurgan culture around six thousand years ago, their heady status as divine symbols in Egyptian and Middle Eastern civilizations, to their present status as dairy and beef machines, as victims of our industrial and technological civilization. And worse was to happen to cows, as Rifkin describes them as modern locusts devouring the land wherever they appear.

The story of western civilization, as Rifkin tells it, is the pursuit of beef protein, yet the value of beef protein was based on a mistake scientists made around 1913 when they observed that newborn laboratory rats grew faster when fed meat than laboratory rats who were not fed meat. Dietitians took up the call for red meat protein for children; no one reckoned on the myriad diseases which too much meat would cause humans. The laboratory rats thrived.

Almost from the dawn of beef history, meat has been associated with virility, health, and military prowess. The Kurgans are the earliest military civilization we know of. Having tamed and learned to ride the horse, they invaded other lands, bringing with them war and the association of cattle with warrior values.

The bull and the horse went on to have extraordinary careers in the conquest of South and North America, from the pampas in Argentina to the grass lands of North America, transforming forests, farms, and pastoral lands into cattle ranges. From godhead to the semi-diseased animal of the factory farm the bull symbolized power and virility, as it still does in the cult of the bull fight.   Signs in butcher shops often show a charging bull with the slogan beneath, "Meat Builds Strength." Yet the bull is a vegetarian animal—as are all the powerful animals—the elephant, the whale, the ox, the buffalo, the rhinoceros. In six thousand years had no one noticed this?   As always there were vested interests in this misreading. As beef became the basis of wealth in England and the United States and a symbol of national power, the association of meat with social status grew. The term, "conspicuous consumption," introduced by the economist Theodore Veblen was used to describe thee appetites of Diamond Jim Brady and Lillian Russell, fabulous Broadway creatures in the early 20th century who were known each to devour a two pound steak at a sitting. The term became a metaphor for western civilization.

Soon the creation of the railroad, the refrigerator, and the freezer sealed the fate of meat consumption, as it now became possible for ordinary people to consume what Brady and Russell ate, and the eating habits of Americans underwent a radical change.

In 1916, *American Meat,* by Dr. Albert Leffingwell, sounded the alarm about the relationship between the rise in the consumption of meat and the rise in cancer. It was ignored, as were his other books on the spread of experimentation on children and animals. Leffingwell's analysis of the problem was interesting, though different from that of such present day doctors as Michael Greger, Nathan Pritikin, Dean Ornish, Milton Mills, Colin Campbell, Caldwell B. Esselstyn, Neal Barnard, Michael Klaper, and others who have traced diseases to our diet. But Leffingwell was among the first to connect the problem of cancer with meat: he went into the slaughterhouses and observed that cows with cancerous tumors were being sent down the kill line. The understanding of metastasis was limited, and the government believed that if you cut out the observably diseased part of an animal, you cut out the disease. The slaughterers would remove the tumors and send the animals on their way to market.

In the 1950's and 1960's, as factory farming and the CAFO system (Confined Animal Feed Operation) became entrenched, with its reliance on hormones and antibiotics, the public became alarmed at the relationship between meat and disease. Rachel Carson sounded a warning in her introduction to Ruth Harrison's book, *Animal Machines: The New Factory Farming Industry,* by Ruth Harrison (1964):

> As a biologist whose special interests lie in the field of ecology, or the relation between living things and their environment, I find it inconceivable that healthy animals can be produced under the artificial and damaging conditions that prevail in these modern factory-like installations, where animals are grown and turned out like so many inanimate objects.....As she (Ruth Harrison) makes abundantly clear, this artificial environment is not a healthy one. Diseases sweep through these establishments, which indeed are kept going only by the continuous administrations of antibiotics.

In 1985, the journalist Orville Schell wrote *American Meat: Antibiotics, Hormones and the Pharmaceutical Farm.* Not a vegetarian, Schell declared that he loved a good hamburger and wanted to know what was going into his. He travelled throughout the country in search of his "good hamburger" and was depressed at what he found. His exposé of antibiotics in meat and its damaging impact on human health was dismaying. But the consumption of meat continued to increase. Americans---the world---could not get enough of the flesh of this ancient god. Outbreaks of e.coli, mad cow disease, and the dizzying increase of cancer rates at first frightened the public, who were then soon consoled by the cheap price of meat or by diversion to eating chicken. In due time, the news leaked out that chickens, also produced in "factory-like installations" bred their own dangers, and all animal products, eggs, cheeses, and milk products were under suspicion. But they were always cheap and easy to get, and "cheap and easy" trumps everything, including our phenomenal health care costs. The dots had yet to be connected.

There were other problems, hidden as usual from the public, the dots between our meat and agricultural industry and our immigration problems. Upton Sinclair was the first to expose this about the Chicago slaughterhouses in his 1906 classic, *The Jungle* (reissued in 1988). But as Americans turned from beef to chicken to avoid problems associated with beef, similar immigration problems overtook the chicken industry, examined in Steve Striffler's book, *Chicken: The Dangerous Transformation of America's Favorite Food* (Yale University Press, 2005). The turkey, America's favorite holiday food, arrives on America's sacred table, a product of poultry porn in the manipulation of its sexual life.

Worse was to come: In 2007 Al Gore was awarded the Noble Peace Prize for his work on the Intergovernmental Panel on Climate Change. As important as this was, neither had Al Gore connected the dots. This was left to another UN agency, The Food and Agriculture Organization, which published the first extensive detailed report in 2006, on what the consumption of meat was doing to the environment. It was called "Livestock's Long Shadow." Its examination of the relationship of our agricultural processes to climate change was often quoted---and often ignored. If rising rates of cancer, salmonella poisoning, the loss of the use of antibiotics in ordinary medicine, outbreaks of e.coli, news of rising e.coli in the Potomac causing fish to die, could not scare the public, why should the news of rising waters, increasing heat waves, the spread of deserts, the drying of wells, the increase of famine---scare them! The determined meat eater could face down and argue away any impending catastrophe. Governments met to find solutions; delegates spent huge sums of money to travel around the world to worry in each other's faces. No one said: "Change the diet, change what we eat and the way we farm. Turn off the meat spigot! We are drowning in poisoned feces and poisoned waters."

There was one group that said it. The vegetarians. They had been saying it for half a century. John Robbins in *The Food Revolution: How Your Diet Can Save Your Life and The World.*

(2001), and many others connected the dots between our moral selves, our diets, and our responsibility to the planet. Many others, too numerous to mention here, ethicists and philosophers, explored the ethics of food and farming.

The vegetarian movement had gotten it right. As Rifkin writes at the end of his book:

> Today, the third stage of the human-bovine saga beckons. By choosing not to eat the flesh of cattle, we serve notice of our willingness to enter into a new covenant with this creature, a relationship that transcends the imperatives of the market and profligate consumption. Freeing the bovine from the pain and indignities suffered in the modern mega-feedlots and in the slaughterhouses is a humane act of great symbolic and practical import....It is an acknowledgement of the damage we moderns have inflicted on the whole of creation in pursuit of unrestrained power over the forces of nature.

The environmental crisis and its relationship to food had entered the intellectual landscape. The problem was not only the bovine, but chicken, fish, water, human population density, and faith in the human power to control all this with technology. The philosopher, Hans Jonas, gave it its elegant moral meaning in his book, written in 1984, *The Imperative of Responsibility.* Technological man, with his power to undo the earth, requires a new ethic.

> The lengthened reach of our deeds moves responsibility, with no less than man's fate for its object, into the center of the ethical stage. Accordingly, a theory of responsibility, lacking so far, is set forth for both the private and the

public sphere. Its axiom is that responsibility is a correlate of power and must be commensurate with the latter's scope and that of its exercise.

The vegetarian movement had gotten it right. Everyone's exercise of power can be manifested in their diets. It is a power everyone has. Vegetarians had not only gotten the problem right, but published dozens of glorious vegetarian books to prove that one could save the environment and eat well. Vegetarian and vegan cookbooks began to rival traditional cookbooks in yearly publications and sales. Vegetarian festivals sprang up around the country. Vegetarian food was available in local supermarkets.

The shift began about thirty years ago with small groups of families who were concerned about the antibiotic-drenched, chemicalized food they were feeding their children. They met in small groups in different homes. Someone found out where organic vegetables and fruits could be bought, and distributed the food to those who "bought in." It was voluntary and small scale. Then CSA's developed (Community Supported Agriculture). The groups were larger and met with local farmers. Most of us were naive about how food grew, how seasons and climate affected food, but we learned. Vegetarians were curious about different foods, they shopped in ethnic markets and ate in ethnic restaurants. The world of food choices became larger. Farmers' Markets appeared, local supermarkets began to feature organic foods, local foods, vegetarian and vegan products. Upscale vegan restaurants where you could get a gourmet vegan meal with a bottle of organic wine appeared. Vegan and vegetarian chefs competed in culinary contests and often won, and vegan restaurants soon became world renowned. This was a trickle up revolution.

The vegetarian movement inaugurated a revolution in our diet, in farming practice, in supermarket purchasing, in the relationship between consumer and market managers. People with food problems "came out of the closet" and spoke up, people with gluten sensitivities, lactose intolerance, celiac disease, and other food related allergy problems. Chefs and cooks had to become more skillful. Instead of the complaint heard several decades ago, "What is there to eat if you don't eat meat," we had created a world of food choices beyond our imagination.

This cookbook is a tribute to the thousands of men and women who ran organizations, to people like Karen Davis of United Poultry Concerns, The Vegetarian Resource Group, the National American Vegetarian Society, Jewish Vegetarians of North America, the Christian Vegetarian Association, the American Vegan Society, the International Vegetarian Union, to Neal Barnard and his work at Good Medicine. The thousands who volunteered at outreach tables, published newsletters and magazines, websites and blogs have remained loyal to a vision of the connection between earth and food and health and survival. The vegetarian movement became one of the most significant movements of the 20th century and beyond. The future thanks you.

There is a Jewish tradition of saying a prayer of thanks when a new holiday or a new custom is inaugurated. Called the Shehechayanu, it is simple: We thank God for allowing us to reach this season, and allowing us to inaugurate this new holiday, and we pray for its future.

Tofu is a great mixer and can accompany many dishes. It is an inexpensive form of protein, which can be used in a variety of recipes, such as tofu loaves, tofu burgers, sloppy joes, stir fries, sweet and sour dishes with green peppers and pineapples. It can be fried, baked, and marinated. One of the virtues of tofu is that it marinates quickly, within 30-60 minutes. Almost any marinade will do, simple tamari or soy sauce, or tamari or soy sauce mixed with tomato sauce or a little vinegar.

Tofu is extraordinarily adaptable and versatile. It can be used in main courses, or to make dips, spreads, dessert creams, and cakes.

With all these virtues, it is also healthy. Soybeans may decrease the risk of colon and rectal cancer, and possibly breast cancer because soybeans contain isoflavin, which seems to prevent estrogen from binding to human cells and forming tumors. However, by itself tofu has little taste, so don't make the mistake of buying a package of tofu and eating it as is. (It isn't harmful to eat that way, it just isn't tasty.) But alas, the majority of soy beans today are genetically altered. If you mind GMO's, read the package labeling.

You can buy 1 pound blocks of tofu in many supermarkets. (Check the expiration date as you would for any food). Tofu is packaged in liquid to keep it moist and fresh. To use, slit the package open and drain well, place in a colander for about 15 minutes, then pat dry with kitchen toweling.

Tofu blocks are available in "firm," "extra firm," "regular," "soft" or "silken" textures. Recipes generally specify which type you will need. Firm and extra firm are the most useful; they contain the least water and hold their shape best in cooking.

Once the package of tofu is opened, it is best to use it up or freeze it. It can be stored in water to cover in a closed container, for about three days in the refrigerator in water to cover. The water should be changed daily. Drained and wrapped well in plastic wrap, it will keep in the freezer for many weeks. It takes about six hours to defrost at room temperature. So plan accordingly. After defrosting, squeeze out remaining moisture with kitchen toweling. Frozen tofu marinates well and adds heft to dishes like chili.

An excellent introduction to the versatility of tofu is *Tofu Cookery*, by Louise Hagler (Book Publishing Company, Summertown, TN 38483).

< 1 >

Tempeh is a cultured food, like yogurt. It is made of a mixture of cooked soybeans and grains, or of soybeans alone, bound together by the fermenting action of a mold. (Spots on the surface are a result of this mold.) It has a nutty, earthy flavor and is higher in protein than tofu. Tempeh is sold frozen or refrigerated. Like tofu, it can be marinated, cubed, sliced, fried, oven fried, used in sandwiches with onions, sauerkraut or ketchup. It makes for a fast, easy sandwich, high in complete protein and if not fried, low in fat. Always keep refrigerated or frozen.

<>

ABOUT GRAINS

Beans and whole grains were the foundation of diets in the past, until about a century ago. Each region had its prized grain from which hundreds of dishes were made. Rice was the grain of the Asian world; wheat, barley, oats and rye of the Middle Eastern world; corn was the basic grain for the North and South American native people; quinoa was the prized grain for the Incas, and sorghum and millet the grains of Africa. Today, we can enjoy the blessings of all these grains. They are making a deserved comeback as nutritionists discover their inestimable contribution to health, and as modern cooks create more and more delicious uses for them. For a history and discussion of grains, a useful book is *Grains for Better Health*, by Maureen B. Keene and Daniella Chace.

It is best to eat whole grains, rather than processed grains, and they should be rinsed thoroughly before cooking. Both grains and beans can be cooked easily in modern pressure cookers. Consult Lorna Sass' books, *Vegetarian Cooking Under Pressure*, or Lorna Sass' *Complete Vegetarian Kitchen* .

Wild rice is actually a grass. When cooked with long or medium grain rice adds a nice texture; also a few wheat berries added to rice gives rice a crunchy texture. If blending rices and/or grains, cook according to directions for the dominant grain.

Basmati rice is a bit more expensive than standard brown rices, but particularly flavorful, and has a wonderful aroma. It should be cooked according to directions for brown rice.

It is economical to buy rices and grains in bulk, but don't stock up on more than you can use in two months. Store in a tightly closed canister or jar on a cool, dark shelf. For convenience, Lorna Sass recommends freezing in labelled Ziploc bags for 4 to 5 months. (Lorna Sass, *Complete Vegetarian*, p. 63) Grains can also be stored in the refrigerator for 4 months. Leftover cooked grains can be reheated in a rice steamer or a double boiler.

< 2 >

Most beans benefit from an overnight presoaking, except for lentils and peas which do not need presoaking. Presoaking can reduce the time needed for cooking by several hours, and some people claim that it reduces the reaction of gassiness. However, gassiness is often a temporary problem, as the digestive system usually adjusts to eating beans. There are also several products now on the market which might help end the problem. Look for a solution without cutting beans from your diet. They are too healthy to forego.

Store beans on a cool, dark, dry shelf, preferably in a glass jar with a tight cover. Beans can be kept for six months; however, they tend to harden and dry as they age and this can affect cooking time.

Drain off the soaking water and cook beans in clean, fresh water, in about double the volume of beans. Bring water to a boil, lower heat to simmer, and cook in a partially covered pot. Most beans swell to 2 1/2 times their dry volume. So cook in a large enough pot. Test one or two beans to see when they are done. Taste or roll them between two fingers. They should be soft, but not mushy. Test for doneness about 1/2 hour before allotted cooking time. Do not add salt to beans until they are finished cooking.

If you make more beans than you need, freeze the remainder without water in a container with a lid. Frozen beans can be kept for 3 months, and you will be a step ahead when you make your next bean dish. You can also freeze them in small containers and use as needed for spreads or in soups. If cooked beans are stored in the refrigerator, however, use within three days.

Always rinse beans thoroughly in a colander even if they are organic, because dust can settle on them.

◇

COOKING WITHOUT EGGS

The following suggestions are from *Instead of Chicken, Instead of Poultry*, by Karen Davis.

< 3 >

Eggs are about 70% fat, and an average egg contains 250 miligrams of cholesterol. Generally, if a recipe calls for only one egg, it can be omitted.

Eggs are used to leaven, bind, and liquefy in baking. Each of the following is for one egg.

1 tablespoon arrowroot powder, 1 tablespoon soy flour + 2 tablespoons water (if needed).

2 Tablespoons flour, 1/2 tablespoon vegetable shortening, 1/2 teaspoon baking powder + 2 tablespoons water.

2 Tablespoons to 1/4 cup tofu, blended with liquid called for in recipe.

2 Tablespoons cornstarch or potato starch.

2 Tablespoons arrowroot flour.

1 heaping Tablespoon soy powder + 2 tablespoons water.

1/2 to 1 banana, mashed.

1 Tablespoon flax seeds + 1/4 cup water. Blend flax seeds and water in blender for 1-2 minutes, till mixture is thick and has the consistency of beaten egg white.

<>

OILS AND VINEGARS

Recipes in this cookbook generally call for olive oil, sesame oil, vegetable oil, or safflower oil, or hot Chinese oil (usually as an option).

Vegetable oils are usually canola, safflower, corn, or a mixture of these. Opinion is often divided about their nutritional and taste merits, and the decision is personal. Vegetable oils are not as healthy as olive oil, but lighter in taste, and many people prefer to sauté in a vegetable oil.

Olive, sesame and grape seed are among the best oils as they have a better ratio of omega 3's and 6's. Caldwell Esselstyn allows no oil in his program. But it is designed for those with serious heart disease and towards reversing it without bypass surgery.

Fat has nine calories per gram while protein and carbs have four. And it is easy to add a lot of fat. Look at recipes carefully and see if you can't eliminate the oil, or reduce it, depending on what it is.   Water sautéeing is a good method, and then add maybe a tablespoon for a large skillet. When baking one needs some oil or your product will taste gummy. But 2 Tablespoons will do for a muffin recipe, not the larger amount usually called for.

< 4 >

Whether sautéeing in vegetable or olive oil, if you are calorie or fat conscious, you can "sweat" your vegetables, by putting a thin layer of oil in the skillet or pot, just enough to cover the bottom, heat a little, then place your vegetables in the pot, mix well to cover vegetables with the oil. After about 2-3 minutes, add a few tablespoons of water to continue cooking the vegetables. Add more water as water boils off, to prevent the vegetables from burning. This method part sautés and part steams the vegetables. The vegetables will taste as if they have been sautéed, but most of the fat has been left out.

The method works well with onions, green beans, green and red peppers, brussel sprouts. With green beans, peppers and brussel sprouts, cover vegetables after water has been added and cook for five to ten minutes, depending on how "limp" or "chewy" you want the vegetable to be.

Olive oil has the greatest nutritional virtues, for it is high in monounsaturated fats, but it can be heavy in taste and it is usually more expensive than vegetable oils. Olive oil lovers feel about olive oil as wine lovers feel about wines. Labels of "Extra Virgin," "Virgin," and "Cold Pressed" can be confusing. "Extra Virgin" indicates that the oil was made from the first pressing of the olive and therefore has the fullest flavor. "Cold pressed" means that the oil has not been refined. "Virgin" refers to the second pressing. Olive oil should be stored in a dark bottle. It can be kept for as long as eighteen months, perhaps two years, if it is not exposed to sunlight. Olive oil is expensive, because gathering the olives is a tedious, time-consuming job, since all the olives in an orchard, even on the same tree, do not ripen at the same time.

Sesame oil has an exotic flavor. A few drops added to other oils for stir-fries, or sprinkled over grated carrots transforms a simple dish. It is often used in Oriental cookery.

The variety of vinegars available is astonishing, and each one can impart a distinctive flavor to your salad or marinade. There is apple vinegar, wine vinegar, white balsamic vinegar, red balsamic vinegar, tarragon vinegar, rice vinegar, brown rice vinegar, apple sage vinegar and herbal vinegars.

The quality and price of these vinegars varies a great deal, so you may have to experiment to find out what you like. Rice vinegar is nicely mild, but if too mild, add a few drops of wine vinegar to it. You can mix mild vinegars with a few drops of a more acerbic vinegar to satisfy your taste.

< 5 >

HERBS, SALADS AND GREEN THINGS

See, I give you every herb, seed, and green thing to you for food.
(Gen. 1:28-30)

When the poet John Keats went to medical college in London at the beginning of the nineteenth century, there was an herbal garden attached to his medical school where he not only learned the medicinal uses of herbs, but drew poetic inspiration. In his time, herbal gardens were still attached to medical schools and doctors were required to know the uses of herbs. Here we are concerned only with herbs as food, but you should explore their health values. Like grains and legumes, herbs are making a sensational comeback, adding luster and zest to our meals. They are the great temptresses of the taste buds. A few basil or sage leaves or some dill will transform your soup or salad. But as with vinegars you must make the choice of what to use and how much. The only requirement with herbs is that they be fresh.

Herbs can change the nationality of your food. Vegetables become Italian vegetables when cooked with garlic, oregano, or thyme; they become Mexican, when cooked with cumin or red pepper; they become Chinese when cooked with curry and ginger. You can sprinkle them on baked potatoes, on bread, on rice, on celery ribs, on sliced tomatoes. You can put them in soups and on salads, and vary the taste of a food each time you use a different herb.

Many of our favorite herbs, like coriander, mustard, dill, aniseeds, caraway, fennel, nutmeg, and poppy come from the seeds of plants. Seeds in general have been valued for their health for centuries. Seeds which are not herbs, like sunflower seeds and sesame seeds, are also healthy, high in protein, but high in fat. These may be sprinkled on foods and in salads, served lightly roasted or plain.

The following is a list of commonly used herbs and suggestions for their use. It is difficult to describe tastes, unless they are distinctively bitter or sweet, so each cook must make the voyage of discovery. Notice which herbs are useful for fruits, desserts, in baking, in salads or in soups, and which herbs pair together or work well together so that each brings out the other's flavor.

Aniseed imparts a licorice flavor to foods, and is interesting to use on fruit desserts. Try it sparingly at first.
Basil is the beloved herb in pasta and Italian dishes, but is equally good in soups, salads and even on grain dishes.
Bay leaves are used mainly in soups and stews, but should be removed before serving the dish.

< 6 >

Cardamon comes in tiny hard seeds, and can be bought whole or ground. Try it on sliced bananas, baked apples, or sweet potato pudding.

Caraway is often used for decorative purposes, but can be tried in cole slaws, potato salads, and noodle dishes.

Cayenne pepper is used in hot spices, curries, chutneys and chilis.

Chives are a sweeter form of onion or scallion. Nice in soups or chopped into salads.

Cilantro: see Coriander. **Tip:** If you find cilantro too strong--cut in half and use half cilantro and half parsley leaves

Cinnamon is possibly the most popular spice used in baking. It combines well with nutmeg and/or sugar for toppings on puddings and baked fruits.

Cloves are also popular in baking and on baked apples and sweet potato puddings, but try them in vegetable stews and chilis for a surprising flavor. Remove before serving.

Coriander is the seed of the cilantro plant, good in soups, bean dishes, curries, and chilis.

Cumin is excellent in Mexican, Indian and Middle Eastern dishes. Many cooks like to mix coriander and cumin together.

Curry can be bought ready-made. Curries vary in quality and you should try to decide which kind appeals to you. A basic curry can be made from a mixture of two teaspoons each of ground coriander, cumin, and turmeric; 1 teaspoon of ground nutmeg, 1/2 teaspoon of salt, 1/4 teaspoon cayenne pepper and freshly ground black pepper, to taste.

Dill is a favorite herb for salads and soups, and for use in pickling.

Fennel also has a licorice flavor, but not as strong as anise. It is used in baking and on fruit desserts.

Garlic is the darling of many cuisines, especially Italian. Its medicinal value has adherents and opponents. It is related to the onion family and can be sautéed together with onions.

Ginger, like curry, is good in Oriental dishes, vegetable stir fries, but also on baked fruit dishes. Use sparingly, since its flavor is usually strong.

Marjoram is similar to oregano, but milder.

Mustard comes in many forms, ground dry, as seeds, and wet. The seeds can be used to combine with curries, ginger and cumin. When using in stir fry vegetables, sauté 1 tablespoon quickly in hot oil until they begin to pop.

Nutmeg combines well with cinnamon, and is good for cooked fruit desserts. Try it sparingly on cooked, pureed broccoli for a surprising flavor.

Paprika is useful on stewing onions for flavor and color. There is also hot paprika, which should be used cautiously, and smoked paprika as well.

Parsley is often used--and wasted--as a garnish. It is wonderful in salads and soups, and for making pesto.

Poppy Seed is often used in noodle dishes.

Rosemary is most often used in tomato-based dishes, but try it in breads, muffins, and simple cakes for a different flavor. It can also be used sparingly in salads and soups.

< 7 >

Sage has a strong flavor, usually recommended for soups, but try it cut up finely on salads. Use sparingly.

Tarragon is used most often in salads, and in vinegars.

Thyme is a dainty herb, used in Italian recipes, and in tomato stews. Sprinkle it on grains and in bean dishes.

Turmeric gives food a dashing yellow color. It is most often used along with ginger and curries.

◇◇◇

A FINAL WORD

Holidays are great times to try out those special recipes you've bypassed all year long. But first read through any recipe you haven't made before. The internet is a great resource for an ingredient that is new to you. Use Wikipedia to find out more about herbs. Make sure your herbs are fresh, leave yourself enough time for whatever you plan, and check that you have all the ingredients beforehand. Ask guests to bring their favorite holiday vegan dish. If they don't have one, send them a recipe from this cookbook. Enjoy the cooking, the learning, as well as the eating.

< 8 >

<<PRESENTATION OF THE HOLIDAY>>

A special holiday dish is often used as the centerpiece. We have selected recipes that can be used this way. If you have a sideboard, it's nice to put the side dishes, breads and muffins on that. If not, place the side dishes around the table.

<ENTRÉES>

For a holiday presentation place the main entrée in the center of the table on a platter, and surround with a variety of stuffed vegetables like eggplants and squashes.

There are several holiday nut loaves in this section which are not only delicious, but can easily be doubled for a large crowd. You can make two without much difficulty or, if you are ambitious, make several different kinds.

There are also some sumptuous one-pot dishes as a variation on the loaf. Serve these in a handsome large bowl and surround with rolls or specialty breads

Hearty Appetite

◇

< 9 >

<< HOLIDAY LOAF >>

This dish is always a holiday favorite because it can feed many guests, can be prepared ahead, keeps well, and leftovers can be served chilled the next day. Fussy, but worth it. Serve leftovers with salsa or vegan gravy.

2 Tablespoons olive oil, divided
1 large onion, diced
1 cup chopped walnuts
1 cup rolled oats (not instant variety)
1/2 pound mushrooms, sliced
2 cups vegetable broth
(vegetable cubes can be used to make broth)
2 cloves garlic, minced
1 cup grated carrot
3 Tablespoons Dijon, or other hearty mustard
4 Tablespoons tomato sauce
2 Tablespoons soy or tamari sauce
1 pound firm tofu, drained well, patted dry
2 Tablespoons arrowroot powder
2 cups whole wheat breadcrumbs,
or other preferred breadcrumbs

Preheat oven to 375 degrees.
In a large skillet, heat 1 Tablespoon oil. Sauté onion until caramelized, about 15 minutes. Stir occasionally. Transfer onions to a large mixing bowl.

In the same skillet, heat remaining oil, add walnuts, and sauté over medium heat 3 minutes. Add oats, sauté another 3 minutes, stirring. Add mushrooms, broth, and garlic. Reduce heat to low. Cook until mushrooms soften and stock is absorbed, about 8 minutes.

While oat mixture cooks, add carrot, mustard, tomato paste or sauce, soy sauce or tamari. Add oat mixture to bowl with onions, and set aside.

Purée tofu and arrowroot powder in blender or food processor until smooth. Add to oat-carrot mixture, and mix well. Add bread crumbs and mix again. Pour into oiled 11 X 5 1/2 loaf pan (approximately). Bake 40 minutes. Cool 30 minutes before slicing.

SERVES 10-12

< 10 >

The next two loaves are similar with slight variations and easy to make. They can be prepared early in the day and popped into the oven in late afternoon. The trick to the first loaf is to baste it often and keep it moist. Use whatever nuts you prefer except peanuts, and do not use salted nuts. A variety of almonds, walnuts, and cashews is best. In order to keep the expense of this dish down, buy nuts on sale in advance, or in bulk and freeze for later use.

Nut loaves are great for holiday dinners, but should be accompanied by something light, like a green salad.

Preheat oven to 350 degrees.

> **1 large onion, finely chopped**
> **3 cloves of garlic, finely chopped**
> **2 large carrots, grated**
> **3 cups of mixed ground nuts**
> **1 cup matzo meal**
> > **or finely ground breadcrumbs**
> **4 Tablespoons tomato paste**
> **1 large onion, sliced thinly**
> **2-1/2 cups vegetable stock**

Mix all ingredients well, except vegetable stock and sliced onion.
Grease an ovenproof baking dish 8 X 8 (or close to that). Cover the bottom of the dish with the sliced onions
Form nut and carrot mixture into a loaf and place on top of sliced onions.

Bake 45 minutes. Baste with vegetable stock every 15 to 20 minutes.
Remove from oven and let cool for ten to fifteen minutes.

Serves 8

Tips: Ingredients can be cut in half for a smaller loaf, but loaf is very good the next day, so don't worry about having too much.

< 11 >

<< VEGETABLE NUT LOAF ll >>

This dish is originally from Freya Dinsha's recipe in her book, *The Vegan Kitchen*. It requires heating in the oven for about ten minutes, because the ingredients are precooked and, like many vegetarian loaves, it will keep well for the next day.

Preheat oven to 350 degrees

Oil for oven dish,
2/3 cups of Brazil nuts
2/3 cups of filberts
water to cover nuts
2 medium potatoes, peeled
2 small zucchini squash
1 medium sweet potato
  (or small butternut squash)
1 large carrot
4 ribs celery
1 small onion
3-1/2 cups water
2-2/3 cups matzo meal
  or finely ground breadcrumbs
1-1/2 teaspoons mixed herbs
4 teaspoons olive oil
2 Tablespoons paprika

Cover nuts with water and simmer about 1 hour until soft
Drain, dry, and grind.
Dice all the vegetables and cook together in 3-1/2 cups water for 30 minutes.
Drain and mash vegetables. Mix in the nuts.
Add the matzoh meal or bread crumbs, oil, and herbs. Mix well.
Put mixture into a 5 X 7 oiled baking pan, press down well. Sprinkle paprika evenly over the top. Bake for 10 minutes.

Serves 4-6, but is easy enough to make two to serve 8-12

Variation: Cover loaf with a mushroom sauce, or with sautéed mushrooms and/or caramelized onions.

< 12 >

<< ALMOND AND PECAN LOAF >>

Zel Allen is, we think, the doyenne of cooking with nuts. Some of her recipes may require a bit more work, but they're always worth it, and what better time to express delight in making an unforgettable dish.

Preheat oven 375 degrees.
Lightly oil a 9-inch spring form pan or a 5 X 8 glass loaf pan.
Line bottom of the pan with parchment paper, or lightly oil

2 onions
1 pound russet potatoes, unpeeled, washed
1 garlic clove, coarsely chopped
2-1/4 teaspoons salt
2 cups whole almonds
1/3 cups walnuts
1/3 cup pecans
1 ripe diced tomato
1/3 cup plus 1 Tablespoon of water
1/4 cup plus 1 Tablespoon nutritional yeast flakes
2 garlic cloves, minced
1/2 teaspoon ground nutmeg
1/4 teaspoon dried basil
1/4 teaspoon dried thyme
1/4 teaspoon dried marjoram
1/4 teaspoon ground pepper
dash of cayenne (optional)
1 large, ripe sliced tomato

Cut onions in half and coarsely chop one half. Pulse chop remaining onions in food processor until minced, transfer to a large bowl.

Cut potatoes into coarse chunks in water to cover. Cook in a 2 quart saucepan with the garlic, onion and salt, cover with water. Cover pot and bring to a boil. Reduce heat and simmer for 10 minutes, or until potatoes are tender. Drain and transfer to a large bowl, mash with a fork, add the reserved minced onion.

Continue

< 13 >

Process the walnuts and pecans in food processor until they are ground, but still a little crunchy. Add to the potatoes and onions.

Add remaining ingredients, except the sliced tomatoes. Mix thoroughly. Spoon into pan, press down with the back of a large spoon to make the mixture compact.

Arrange tomato slices on the top. Bake 50-60 minutes.
Remove from oven, let cool 15 minutes.
Loosen edges of the loaf with a flatware table knife.
If using a springform pan, release sides of pan. Otherwise, ease loaf out of pan gently, by running a flat edge knife around the edges.
Cut into wedges or slices.

Serves 6-8

◇

Nuts are among the most diverse and adaptable of foods, easy to store and to keep. In past ages, when humans went through cycles of feast or famine, they depended on stored nuts to get them through the famine. Unshelled nuts keep indefinitely without having to be pickled, marinated, or smoked. They are among the most dependable of foods and have been found in almost every civilization–going back to the Stone Age. The squirrel knows what it's doing. But beware: nuts are fattening—that's why the squirrel keeps hopping.

◇

< 14 >

<< A NUT TORTE >>

This elegant torte also comes from the wonderful cookbook, *The Nut Gourmet,* by Zel Allen who, along with her husband, runs the website, Vegans in Paradise. This dish is a terrific combination of wild rice, mushrooms, nuts and sage. You will need a 9-inch spring form pan, lightly oiled and lined with parchment paper. Though a bit complicated, it can be prepared the day before, stored in the refrigerator, and reheated at 350 degrees for 15-20 minutes, which makes the cooking easier.

Heat oven to 375 degrees

2-3/4 cups water plus a separate 1/3 cup water
2/3 cups wild rice
2-1/8 teaspoons salt
3/4 pounds potatoes, red or white, cut into 1-inch cubes
1/2 cup coarsely chopped pecans
1/4 cup coarsely chopped walnuts
1-14 ounce package of vegan ground sausage (Field Roast Sausage package)
4 large portobello mushrooms, chopped
1 large onion, diced
2 Tablespoons olive oil
2 teaspoons poultry seasoning
1/4 teaspoon ground pepper
1/2 teaspoon Hickory liquid smoke
2 ripe tomatoes, sliced

Combine 1-3/4 cups of water, wild rice and 3/4 teaspoon of salt in a 2 quart saucepan. Cover, bring to boil, reduce heat, simmer 45-50 minutes. Drain excess liquid and set aside.

Combine potato cubes, 1 cup of water, pinch of salt, and cook approximately 10 minutes or until potatoes are tender. Drain and mash.

Toast pecans and walnuts in oiled skillet over high heat. Stir constantly 1-2 minutes. Remove to a dish to cool.

Continue

< 15 >

Combine vegan sausage, mushrooms, onions, remaining 1/3 cup water, olive oil, poultry seasoning and pepper in a deep skillet, cook on high heat 5-7 minutes until onions are transparent. Stir frequently with wooden spoon to break up the sausage. Drain and set aside excess liquid. Add remaining 1-1/4 teaspoons salt and Hickory liquid smoke to sausage mixture and mix well.

Add mashed potatoes, toasted nuts and wild rice to this mixture, and mix well.

Press the mixture into the spring form pan, arrange tomato slices over the top. Bake uncovered for one hour. Allow to cool 15-20 minutes before removing from the pan.

To release from pan, run a clean flat edge knife around the edge of pan to loosen the spring form collar. Place the base with the torte on a platter to serve.

Serves 6-8

Mushroom Sauce

2 cups of sliced button mushrooms
1-3/4 cups water plus 3 Tablespoons
1/4 cup soy sauce
1/4 cup dry red wine
2 Tablespoons freshly squeezed lemon or lime juice
3 Tablespoons cornstarch

Combine first four ingredients in a 2 quart saucepan, bring to a boil, turn heat down, simmer for 5 minutes.

Combine cornstarch and remaining 3 Tablespoons. Add this paste to bubbling sauce a little at a time. Stir constantly for about a minute until sauce has thickened to desired consistency.

Serve in a gravy boat or small pitcher. This sauce has many uses. Try it with any of the nut loaves.

< 16 >

Like so many recipes that originally had meat in them, this Transylvanian goulash proves that vegetarian versions are every bit as tasty as the others. This one is adapted from a recipe served by Emma Kende, a Budapest native. When Roberta Schiff says of the paprika "use only this kind," she means "use only this kind." But you can cheat, and the dish will still be great.

1 - 28 oz. jar sauerkraut, drained
1 medium cabbage, sliced, use all but the core
5 or 6 medium fresh tomatoes
1-15 oz. can diced tomatoes or 2 cans of tomatoes instead
1 medium to large onion, diced
2 Tablespoons sweet Hungarian paprika (use only this kind)
2 Tablespoons caraway seeds
2 cloves garlic, chopped
2-3 Tablespoons olive oil
Juice of 1 lemon
2 bay leaves

Sauté the onion and garlic in the olive oil until they gently turn color, transfer to a large pot, add the sauerkraut, paprika, mix together. Add the rest of the ingredients, stir well and let simmer about an hour until the flavors blend well. After it has been simmering about 15 minutes, taste and add more paprika, as needed.

Rinse two cups of long grain brown rice, (jasmine is nice, but any kind of brown rice will do.) Bring three cups of water to a boil, add 1 teaspoon sea salt, then the rice, stir until the water returns to a boil, then cover and simmer for 35 minutes. The heavier the pot the better the rice will cook. A flame deflector under the pot is good for cooking grain. After 35 minutes, turn off the flame and wait another 10 minutes to open the lid and stir. Serve over rice or vegan noodles.

Serves 10

< 17 >

<< CROCKPOT GOULASH >>

Great for a small crowd and for the cook with more time in the morning than in the evening. The aroma from this dish will make it smell like a holiday kitchen. Robin Robertson suggests a 4 quart cooker for the following recipe.

2 Tablespoons olive oil
1 pound tempeh, cut into 1/2 inch slices
1 small yellow onion, halved and thinly sliced
2 cups sauerkraut, drained and rinsed
One 14.5 ounce can of diced tomatoes, drained
1 Tablespoon sweet Hungarian pepper
1/4 cup dry white wine
1 teaspoon caraway seeds (optional)
2 Tablespoons tomato paste
4 or 5 large carrots, quartered
1 1/2 cup vegetable stock
salt and freshly ground pepper to taste
1/2 cup vegan sour cream

Heat 1 Tablespoon of oil in a large skillet over medium heat. Add tempeh, brown for ten minutes. Remove to a dish and set aside.
Do not clean skillet.
Add remaining Tablespoon of oil over medium heat, add the sliced onion, cover and cook about five minutes, until softened.

Transfer onions to crockpot. Add the tempeh and the rest of the ingredients, except the tofu sour cream. Cover and cook on low for 6 hours.

Before serving, drain off 1/2 cup of liquid from the crockpot, mix with tofu sour cream, whisk together. Stir liquid back into the goulash and serve over flat noodles.

Serves 6

Tip: tempeh is best if marinated for a few hours in red wine, soy sauce and a little olive oil. Good for other recipes as well. Serve over flat vegan noodles.

< 18 >

This is a dish that can be as versatile as your imagination. It can be made with a variety of ingredients, and be as simple or as complex as you like. The beauty of this dish is that you can make the stroganoff with all kinds of vegetables or browned tofu. It can hardly be ruined, but stroganoffs are best eaten on the day they are made. Below is a favorite mixture.

Basic Recipe
1 Tablespoon olive oil to oil skillet
1 large onion sliced and sautéed
1/2 head cauliflower, florets steamed 10 minutes
1-1/2 cups halved button mushrooms
pinch salt
1 teaspoon powdered ginger, or 1/2 teaspoon of grated fresh ginger
1 Tablespoon curry powder
1 Tablespoon Hungarian paprika
2/3 cup vegan sour cream

Sauté onions, mix with ginger and curry powders
Add halved mushrooms, sauté until softened, add steamed cauliflower. Mix well.
Add vegan sour cream just before removing from heat, mix again thoroughly.
Add more ginger and curry to taste, mix.

Serve over flat noodles or rice.

Variation: Add or substitute for the cauliflower marinated and browned large cubed tofu pieces. Leave a few minutes extra for this, remove the tofu pieces to a hot plate, and add back into skillet after the onions have been sautéed, or after the mushrooms have softened.

Tip: Tofu is best if marinated first too. See Tips for Tofu

Serves 6. Recipe can be increased to serve 8 or 10.

< 19 >

<<LENTIL LOAF>>

For vegans who are allergic to soy or nuts, lentils make nice roasts and are especially welcome. There are many versions of lentil loaf, but we like this one offered by The Vegetarian Resource Group because it keeps well for the next day and can be served cool or at room temperature.

Begin with 2 cups lentils (1 cup uncooked) cooked according to directions on package. Rinse before cooking.

2 cups tomato sauce
1/2 cup onions, chopped
1/2 cup celery, chopped
3/4 cup rolled oats
1/2 teaspoon garlic powder
1/4 teaspoon Italian seasoning
1/4 teaspoon celery seed
Pepper and salt to taste
1/2 cup walnuts, chopped (optional)

Preheat oven to 350 F.
Mix all ingredients together in a large bowl. Press into lightly oiled, 5 1/2" x 11" loaf pan.

Bake 45 minutes.

Cool slightly, 5-8 minutes. Slice.

Serves 8.

◇

< 20 >

The virtue of lentils cannot be overemphasized. Here is a great way to make a lentil loaf that looks festive and that is almost as easy to make as lentil soup.

Preheat oven to 350 degrees

2 cups uncooked lentils
1/2 cup onions, chopped
1/2 cup celery chopped
3/4 cup rolled oats
1/4 cup of freshly grated ginger
1/2 teaspoon salt
2 large mangos, cubed
1 -1/2 cups of fresh peaches, sliced
1 cup dried cranberries

Rinse and prepare lentils as if for soup, but use only enough water to cover. If you have too much water after cooking, drain.

Add the next 6 ingredients, and mix well in a large bowl. Press into an oiled 5 X 8 loaf pan

Bake 45 minutes. Cool slightly

Arrange the peaches around the circumference of the loaf, and scatter the cranberries inside the center.

Serves 10

Tip: If peaches are not available in your area, use oranges cut in chunks.

< 21 >

Here is another adaptation from a recipe from Zel Allen's book, *The Nut Gourmet*. Best made the day before because the taste improves with standing. Great harvest dish with broccoli, tomatoes, red and yellow peppers.

Preheat oven to 375 degrees.
Lightly oil a 9 X 13 inch glass baking dish.

1-1/2 cups water, plus 1/4 cup
1 cup quinoa
1 teaspoon salt
1/2 pound button mushrooms sliced
1 broccoli crown, chopped
1 red pepper, chopped or minced, but not too fine
1 small onion, chopped
1/2 yellow pepper, chopped---not too fine
2/3 cup walnuts, coarsely ground
2 ripe Roma tomatoes, diced
1/3 cup pine nuts
1/4 cup oat bran or wheat germ
2 garlic cloves, minced
1 teaspoon ground cumin
1 teaspoon ground coriander
1 teaspoon chili powder
1/2 teaspoon salt
1 Tablespoon flax seeds

Combine first three ingredients in a 2 quart saucepan, cover and bring to a boil. Lower heat and cook for 15 minutes until all liquid is absorbed and little rings have formed inside the grains of quinoa.

Combine the next five ingredients and 1/4 cup of remaining water in a large skillet. Cook 2-3 minutes or until just tender. Transfer vegetables to a large bowl. .

Continue

< 22 >

Combine 2 cups of the cooked quinoa in a bowl (refrigerate remaining quinoa for future use) with the walnuts, tomatoes, pine nuts, oat bran, garlic, cumin, coriander, chili powder and salt, mix well.

Spoon the mixture into the baking dish, pack it down, bake uncovered 35-45 minutes. Let cool 10 minutes, then cut into squares.

Serves 6-8

For leftovers, warm the next day in the oven at 350 degrees for 15 minutes.

Zel recommends a Lemon Dill Silken Sauce or a Miso Mayo Sauce to go with this loaf, both easy to make and can be made ahead of time.

Lemon Dill Sauce

Combine 1 12 ounce box of soft silken tofu with 1-3 Tablespoons freshly squeezed lemon juice, 1 teaspoon salt, in teaspoon minced fresh dill weed, or about 1/4 teaspoon dried dill and 1/8 teaspoon freshly ground pepper in a food processor. Process for about 1 minute and store in a covered container in the refrigerator. Will keep for 5 days.

Miso Mayo Sauce

1/2 cup coarsely chopped cashews, ground in food processor to a fine meal
1 cup of vegan mayonnaise
3 Tablespoons freshly squeezed lemon juice
3 Tablespoons of white miso
1 garlic clove
1/4-1/2 teaspoon salt
Dash of freshly ground pepper
Dash of cayenne

Add remaining ingredients to the ground cashews, process until smooth. Serve immediately or chill well. Will keep in covered container in the refrigerator for 1 week.

< 23 >

<<GARDEN LOAF WITH APRICOT GLAZE>>

Glazing this loaf is like icing a cake.

Preheat the oven to 350 degrees   Lightly oil a glass bread loaf pan.

Extra virgin olive oil
1 cup chopped onions- red or sweet
2 cups chopped Baby Bella or Cremini mushrooms
2 cloves garlic, minced
1 Tablespoon balsamic vinegar
5 cups loosely packed baby spinach leaves
Sea salt and ground pepper to taste
1 cup cooked quinoa
1 cup toasted breadcrumbs*
2 Tablespoons Annie's Organic Ketchup
2 Tablespoons molasses
1 Tablespoon olive oil
1 Tablespoon dried Italian seasoning
1 teaspoon fresh minced rosemary
3-4 scallions (spring onions) sliced thin, white to light green section
1 baked sweet potato, peeled, diced (bake about 45 minutes)

Heat the olive oil in a skillet and cook the onion until it is translucent. Add the mushrooms and garlic; stir until softened. Add the balsamic vinegar and stir. Add the spinach. Season with sea salt and ground pepper. Stir and cook down until the mixture is soft, about seven minutes or so.

Spoon the skillet vegetables into a food processor bowl and pulse to make a grainy mixture. Don't over-process-- you want some texture.

Put mixture into a large bowl. Add the cooked quinoa, breadcrumbs, ketchup, molasses and olive oil. Stir to combine. Add rosemary, scallions, dried herbs, and mix well. Keep mixture moist so that it holds together when pressed with a spoon. Add more ketchup as needed to hold mixture together.

Fold in diced sweet potato.
Spoon the loaf mixture into the oiled loaf pan and shape it with moist fingers. Press it tight into the pan. Smooth the top.

* **Tip**: Gluten-free bread or cracker crumbs also work well.

Continue

< 24 >

APRICOT GLAZE

1/4 cup apricot fruit spread (fruit juice sweetened)
1 Tablespoon balsamic vinegar
1 Tablespoon pure maple syrup
A sprinkle of cinnamon and ginger
Hot red chili flakes, to taste

Combine all ingredients.
Pour the glaze over top of the loaf.

Tent loosely with a piece of foil. Bake in the center of a preheated oven until heated through and the edges of the glaze bubble---about 25 to 30 minutes.

Allow loaf to set for ten minutes under foil tent, which will make it easier to slice. Lift out portions with thin spatula.

Makes eight good slices, depending on how you cut it

The apricot seem to have originated in Peking over 4,000 years ago. It is a fragile fruit, and grows best in a temperate climate. The apricot tree migrated from China to Mesopotamia where it was a feature in the hanging gardens of Babylon. It arrived in Italy during the time of Nero in the first century. The Babylonian-Assyrian name for the apricot was "armanu," which seems to mean "the early ripening Persian fruit." The Persians also called apricots "the eggs of the sun"----a marvelous metaphor!

< 25 >

<<BEAN CORN AND TAMALE PIE>>

A dish so resonant with harvest food, you can taste the autumn in it, and a great dish if you live in the southwest---not everyone lives in New England! See Corn Mushroom Torte for an accompanying dish.

Advance Preparation Tip: Make the vegetable mixture, without the corn, a day or two ahead. Add corn just before baking.

1 large green pepper, chopped
1 onion, chopped
2 cloves garlic, minced
1 1/2 tablespoons olive oil
3/4 cup chopped pitted black olives
3 1/2 cups whole canned tomatoes,
           with some of their juice
1-1/2 Tablespoons chili powder, or to taste
1/4 teaspoon red pepper sauce, optional
1 teaspoon salt
1/8 teaspoon freshly ground black pepper
2 -1/2 cups cooked kidney or pinto beans
2-1/2 cups whole kernel corn
1-1/2 cups cornmeal
4-1/2 cups water, divided
3/4 teaspoon salt
1/2 cup breadcrumbs, optional

In 10" or 12" skillet, heat the oil and sauté the green pepper and onion until onion is translucent and green pepper is limp, stirring occasionally. Add garlic and sauté one minute. Add tomatoes, breaking them up with a wooden spoon.

Add the beans, and mash them coarsely with a potato masher. Add olives, chili powder, pepper sauce, salt and pepper. Add enough juice from tomatoes to create a stew-like mixture that is moist, but not too soupy. Reduce heat and simmer, covered 15 minutes.

Meanwhile, boil 2 1/4 cups water in a 2 quart saucepan.

Continue

< 26 >

Mix cornmeal with 1-1/2 cups cold water and 3/4 teaspoon salt. Add to boiling water, stirring constantly. Cook, stirring frequently over medium heat until thickened, about 15 to 20 minutes.

Preheat oven to 350 degrees.

Oil a 13" x 9" X 2" baking dish and spread the cooked cornmeal over its bottom and sides.

Add the corn kernels to the vegetable mixture, stir well, and spoon into the crust.
Sprinkle with breadcrumbs, if desired. Bake 30 minutes.

Serves 8-10.

Corn was often another word for grain, but corn as we know it is one of the ancient foods of civilization---in this case the Native people of Mexico, North and South America who regarded corn as the "gift of the gods," because so many diverse foods and drinks could be made from it. The food was regarded almost as holy in some cultures and ritual dances were performed in honor of it.

However, today, because of genetic manipulation, corn has become controversial.

< 27 >

<<CURRIED TOFU TERRINE >>

A little work, but what can beat a yummy fancy terrine for a holiday dish, adapted from Zel Allen's *The Nut Gourmet.*

2 medium-size red potatoes, unpeeled, coarsely shredded
2 medium-sized carrots, peeled and coarsely shredded
1/2 cup coarsely ground walnuts
3 scallions or green onions, minced
1 small onion, shredded
1/2 cup water
salt and pepper to taste
1 pound extra firm tofu
1 Tablespoon plus 1 teaspoon rice vinegar
1 Tablespoon plus 1 teaspoon freshly squeezed lemon juice
1-1/2 teaspoons curry powder
1-1/4 teaspoons salt
1/4 teaspoon ground pepper
3-4 arugula leaves

Preheat oven to 375 degrees.
Oil a 9 X 5 inch glass loaf pan. Oil bottom of the loaf pan, sprinkle the walnuts and 1/3 of the green onions over the bottom of the loaf pan.

Combine the potatoes and carrots, onion and water in a large skillet, over high heat, stir frequently 15-20 minutes. Sprinkle with salt and pepper.

Combine remaining ingredients except for the arugula leaves in a food processor and process until smooth. Press half of this tofu mixture into the loaf pan over the walnuts and scallions.

Spread the carrot and potato filling over the tofu. Top with remaining tofu and spread evenly over the loaf. Bake 30 minutes, cool 10 minutes at room temperature.

Continue

< 28 >

Loosen with a flatware table knife run around the edges of the pan, and unmold on to a platter. Garnish top with shredded arugula leaves.

Best to use a serrated knife when serving so that the portions will not fall apart.

Serves 6

Tip: Can be prepared in advance and then reheated at 350 degrees for 15 minutes. Flavor improves if made the day before or in the morning. Can also be served with lemon dill sauce.

< 29 >

For an adventurous holiday, try this layered torte adopted from Betty Fussell's book, *Crazy for Corn*. Visit a Mexican market for some of the ingredients.

Preheat oven to 325 degrees. Lightly oil a large baking pan.

4-6 Tablespoons of olive oil
2 medium onions chopped fine
2 cloves garlic, minced
3 tomatoes, chopped to make about 2 cups
2 roasted jalapeno chiles,* seeded and chopped
2 cups washed and chopped mushrooms (not too fine)
1 Tablespoon dried epazote #
1 teaspoon dried thyme
1 teaspoon salt
1/2 teaspoon freshly ground black pepper
16 corn tortillas, 5-1/2 inches round
3/4 pound good vegan cheese, grated

Heat oil in heavy skillet
Saute´onions and garlic 4-6 minutes until soft
Add the tomatoes, mushrooms, and seasoning. Simmer for about 10 minutes until liquid has evaporated.
Put four tortillas in bottom of baking pan, spread with 1/2 the mixture. Sprinkle 1/3 of grated cheese. Repeat with four more tortillas, remaining mixture and 1/3 of the grated cheese. Top with remaining tortillas and remaining cheese.

*To prepare the jalapeno chile, char their skins over a gas flame or under a broiler. Turn to char evenly. Remove skins and stems, and cut chiles open to remove seeds.

epazote is a tea leaf

Continue

< 30 >

4 poblano chiles, prepared same as jalapeno chiles
2 cups tofu sour cream

Pureé poblano chiles with tofu cream in a blender until smooth. Pour 1/2 the sauce over the tortillas. Cover pan tightly with foil and bake for 10-15 minutes.

Remove foil. Cut each stack in half or quarters. Place a portion on each plate, pour remaining sauce over top of each portion.

Serves 8-12

The Native American Harvest festival revolved around the celebration of harvesting the corn, also called the Green Corn Festival or Ceremony. This ceremony is usually held at the full moon in October, when the first corn crop was deemed ready to harvest. Many foods were made from the corn and eaten at the feast, such as corn soup, roast corn, corn bread, corn tortillas.

Today it is difficult to find corn in the United States that has not been genetically modified. In the factory farming system corn is one of the cow's chief foods because it is cheap and grows in such abundance in the United States, but it is a food which is alien to the cow's system and causes it to sicken with much gaseous bloating. The cow evolved to eat grass--not corn. Corn is not adaptable to the cow's system of chewing "its cud twice."

< 31 >

FROM THE SOUL OF THE EARTH:

◇

<< VEGETABLE AND GRAIN DISHES >>

<<STUFFINGS AND STUFFED VEGETABLES>>

< 32 >

Squash makes a great stuffing for many traditional dishes, such as ravioli. It is succulent, and this stuffed cabbage dish is excellent for a large company dinner and keeps well for the next day.

Preheat oven to 350 degrees

One large head of green cabbage, washed
4-5 cups of cooked mashed butternut squash
Oil for a 9 X 12 baking dish with cover
1 large cup of walnuts, chopped
2 teaspoons nutmeg
Pinch of salt

Remove outer leaves of cabbage. Put in boiling water for 5 minutes to soften. Remove promptly.
Bake squash about 45 minutes or until soft. Remove from oven when done, cut in half, clean out seeds and pulp, and mash the squash. Do not mash in a food processor. You don't want this too fine.

Add the chopped walnuts and cinnamon to the squash.
Gently pull away the large outer leaves of cabbage. Place a large Tablespoon of squash in each leaf, roll up, pin sides together, and place in baking dish.

Sauce
One 16 ounce can of plain tomato sauce
3 Tablespoons mild vinegar, or to taste
1-1/2 Tablespoons ground cinnamon
1 cup raisins (optional)
Zest from one orange
4 Tablespoons brown sugar

Mix the ingredients for the sauce and pour over the stuffed cabbage. Bake for 20 minutes. Remove, cover dish to prevent the sauce from drying out.

Serves 8-10

< 33 >

The virtue of a slow cooker for holiday cooking, aside from its health and taste benefits, is that it allows you to make a dish in the morning, and set it aside until 6-8 hours later. It also frees up room on the stove top and in the oven.

Robin Robertson's book, *Fresh from the Vegetarian Slow Cooker,* has a great variety of stuffings and stuffed vegetables that can be cooked in a slow cooker. Here are a few examples: For Wild Mushroom Stuffing, Robertson suggests using a variety of mushrooms to intensify the flavor.

Use a 4 quart slow cooker

1/4 cup dried porcini mushrooms
1 cup boiling water
2 Tablespoons olive oil
1 medium yellow onion, chopped
1 celery rib, chopped
4 ounces cremini mushrooms, coarsely chopped
4 ounces oyster mushrooms, coarsely chopped
1 teaspoon dried thyme
1 teaspoon ground sage
8 cups bread cubes, 1/2 inch size
2 Tablespoons minced fresh parsley leaves
1 teaspoon salt
1 teaspoon ground, black pepper--or to taste
1 teaspoon salt, or to taste
1/4 teaspoon ground pepper
About a scant 1-1/2 cups vegetable stock

Soak the dried porcini in boiling water for 30 minutes. Drain. Reserve and set aside 1/2 cup of liquid.

Rinse the mushrooms and chop them.

Continue

< 34 >

Heat oil in a large skillet over medium heat. Add the onions and celery, cook about 5 minutes, until softened. Add the rest of the mushrooms, thyme and sage, stir to coat.

Transfer vegetables to slow cooker, add bread cubes, parsley, salt and pepper. Stir in the soaking liquid that was set aside, and enough stock to moisten. Smooth out the top of the mixture so there are no lumps, cover, and cook on the low setting 3-4 hours.

Serves 8

There are perhaps about 50, 000 different kinds of mushrooms, but only about 2,000 different kinds are eaten throughout the world. Who eats what in the mushroom world depends on local habits, prices, availability, etc. The French, who are known for their culinary esprit, eat about eighty different kinds of mushrooms. Great Britain and the United States are considered under-privileged when it comes to mushrooms, consuming perhaps only five or six different kinds.

Many people confuse toadstools with mushrooms---they do look alike, which can get people into trouble. Not all toadstools are poisonous, and some mushrooms are. But there is only one mushroom which produces instant death---the amanita, and several which are considered to be hallucinogenic. Hence, the legend that hostile lilliputians live under mushroom caps.

< 35 >

The combination of cranberries and walnuts is always delicious. Cooked slowly 3-4 hours, it becomes as Robin Robertson calls it "a symphony of textures and flavors."

2 Tablespoons of olive oil
1 medium yellow onion, chopped
1 celery rib, chopped
1 teaspoon dried thyme
1 teaspoon ground sage
2 Tablespoons brandy
8 cups of 1/2 inch bread cubes
1 cup chopped walnuts (not too fine)
1/2 cup sweetened dried cranberries
1/4 cup minced fresh parsley
1 teaspoon salt
1 teaspoon ground black pepper
1 -1/2 cups vegetable stock

Heat oil in large skillet over medium heat.

Add onion and celery. Cover, cook 5 minutes or until softened.

Add thyme and sage, stir to coat. Stir in the brandy and cook for one more minute.

Transfer mixture to a 4-quart slow cooker. Add bread cubes, walnuts and cranberries, parsley and seasonings.

Stir in enough stock just to moisten. Mix thoroughly. Adjust seasonings. Add more stock if needed, to moisten the mixture. Cover. Cook on low 3-4 hours. Serve hot.

Serves 8

< 36 >

Many people include mashed potatoes as part of their holiday offering. With only a little extra effort, you can serve this delightful potato casserole.

Preheat oven to 375 degrees.

> 2 Tablespoons oil
> 4 cups sliced mushrooms (about 1 pound)
> 2 cups chopped onions
> 1/2 cup slivered almonds
> 1/2 cup golden raisins
> Salt and pepper
> 8 medium redskin potatoes, boiled and peeled
> 2 teaspoons ground cumin
> 1/2 teaspoon ground turmeric
> 1-3 Tablespoons warm water, stock,
>   or reserved potato cooking water
> 2 Tablespoons margarine, melted

Heat 2 Tablespoons oil in 10" or 12" skillet.
Sauté onions and mushrooms until onions are tender and mushrooms give up their liquid. (You may need to cover the skillet for part of the cooking time, especially if you are using a 10" skillet.) Add raisins, almonds, and a sprinkling of salt.

Oil an 8 cup casserole, about 7" x 11", or 8" x 8"

Mash potatoes, adding 1 Tablespoon or more of warm liquid if necessary to make the potatoes workable. Season with cumin, turmeric, salt and pepper, and add most of the melted margarine.

Place a layer of mashed potatoes in the bottom of casserole. Cover it with mushroom mixture.

Continue

< 37 >

Top with the rest of the potatoes, and brush with remaining margarine.

Bake for about 40 minutes.

Serves 8.

Variation: If you do not want to use cumin, flavor potatoes with a small chopped onion sautéed in melted margarine or oil, but use turmeric for its rich golden color.

Tip: If you add add shredded sautéed tofu on top, or a side dish of sautéed tofu triangles for protein, this can also be served as an entrée and will serve 8-10.

The Versatile Potato Salad

We tend to think of potato salad as picnic food--which it is---and very good picnic food--but it is also great food for a buffet dinner, or for a crowd.

You can make everyday potato salad special by adding a bunch of fresh chopped arugula leaves, or basil leaves. If you like it, include cilantro.

Also consider including any one or all of the following

1-2 tomatoes, cut into eighths.

pitted olives cut in halves

1-2 red peppers. seeded and mildly roasted

◇

< 38 >

This takes potato salad out of the humble picnic category to a whole new domain of elegance.

Preheat oven to 425 degrees.

Step one

Spray of oil
2 pounds red potatoes, quartered (don't peel them)
1 red bell pepper, diced large
2 Tablespoons olive oil
1 teaspoon salt
1 small red onion, diced small

Spray a baking sheet with the oil. Toss the potatoes and the bell pepper with the oil and salt and spread out in one layer. Roast until tender, about 30-40 minutes, stirring frequently. Check for doneness. When done, toss with the onions.

Step two

1 Tablespoon lime juice
1/2 teaspoon salt
Pinch of cayenne pepper
1/2 teaspoon cumin
1/2 teaspoon coriander
2 teaspoons curry powder
2 garlic cloves, minced
3 Tablespoons olive oil

Combine lime juice and salt together. Whisk in remaining ingredients. Pour over potato mixture and mix well to combine.
Roast in oven for 2 or 3 minutes to intensify the flavors.
Remove. Add more salt to taste.

Serves 6

Tip: For a larger company recipe, double ingredients in step one, but only increase ingredients in step two by 50%

< 39 >

What would a harvest celebration be without root vegetables? This one, adapted from Dara Goldstein's book, *The Vegetarian Hearth*, makes use of any vegetables that turn you on. Choose at least six from the following, keeping in mind a blend of tastes and colors. All you need is a large shallow baking dish or casserole. Easy to make and beautiful to look at.

Preheat oven to 425 degrees. Use convection setting, if you have it.

**2 pounds of beets, cooked for 5-7 minutes, cooled
and peeled under cold water
3 large carrots, scraped and cut into large chunks
3 garlic cloves, peeled and left whole
2 large onions, peeled and quartered
3 medium-size potatoes, quartered
2 medium size sweet potatoes, peeled and quartered
2 parsnips, scrubbed and cut into thick slices
One winter squash peeled, seeded, and sliced
2 turnips, peeled and sliced
3 Tablespoons of olive oil*
1 Tablespoon of balsamic vinegar*
1 teaspoon of each of the following: ground pepper, dried summer savory,
dried thyme**

Mix the vegetables with the oil and vinegar, roast in oven for about 45 minutes until vegetables are tender. Turn occasionally.
*It is easy to increase this dish or add other vegetables, but keep in mind certain proportions: Dara Goldstein suggests using two teaspoons of oil and 1 teaspoon of vinegar for each pound of vegetables.

Serves 8

Tip: This dish can be even further enriched with a mustard sauce, made from 2 Tablespoons Earth Balance®, 1 Tablespoon all-purpose flour, 1-1/2 teaspoons dry mustard, 1 cup vegetable broth, 2 Tablespoons Dijon mustard, pinch each of ground pepper and paprika. Whisk flour into melted Earth Balance®. Cook for 1 minute, mix in the dry mustard, whisk in the vegetable broth. Bring to a boil and simmer until sauce thickens. About 5 minutes. Add mustard and seasonings.

< 40 >

BEETS, LEEKS, TURNIPS

ROASTED BEETS

Like leeks, beets are a nuisance to clean because their red color runs over everything, but like leeks they are worth the effort and--again--like leeks, they have so much flavor of their own, they require almost nothing else, and their colors make any table look good.

Preheat oven 350 degrees

3 medium-size beets (peel as in previous recipe)
clean and quarter or cut in eighths
place in heavy casserole dish with cover
drizzle lightly with oil
Sprinkle with 1 heaping Tablespoon of thyme
Bake half an hour, test for done-ness

Serves 4-6, but easy enough to increase the volume---just add more beets and more thyme

Note: Beets are often hard to cut. Clean, then bake for about 20 minutes. Remove from oven and then cut. Turn leftovers into hash brown beets. A yummi alternative to hash brown potatoes, or mix with potatoes or a potato-beet hash.

Variations: Cut cooked beets into smaller pieces and sauté in light oil until crisp, or lay out on an oiled cookie tray and bake 20 minutes until crisp. Or chop up cold and put in green salad. The colors are beautiful.

◇

< 41 >

<< OVEN FRIED OR OVEN-ROASTED TURNIPS >>

Cover a cookie tray with parchment paper. Use convection oven, if you have one. Serve the same day as cooked. Might be limp if kept for the next day.

2 Tablespoons olive oil
5-6 small purple top turnips

Heat oven to 375 degrees

Scrub, peel, and slice turnips thin as you would potatoes. Toss turnip slices in small amount of olive oil and place on parchment paper. Bake for 30 minutes.

Tip: Fresh, small turnips usually do not have to be peeled. If greens look fresh, don't discard, cook as you would any other leafy green.

Serves 5-6

<< OVEN-BAKED LEEKS >>

Leeks are a great discovery to cook with: they add flavor to almost any dish and will often eliminate the need for salt. The only problem with leeks is that they are a nuisance to clean. Dirt gets down inside the tightly wound leaves, and needs strong flushing with water. This recipe is incredibly easy to make---except for the cleaning, but worth it: the dish requires no seasoning, and is a great accompaniment to loaves.

2-3 medium-size leeks
2 Tablespoons olive oil

Heat oven to 350 degrees

Wash leeks carefully by slitting each leek down its length, almost to the end. Spread the leaves and wash with forcefully running water.

Lightly oil a rectangular or oval casserole dish.

Cut leeks in quarters lengthwise, and then in half.

Place in baking dish, lightly sprinkle oil over the leeks, cover, bake 20-25 minutes.

Serves 5-6

< 42 >

Parsnip is an overlooked, healthy root vegetable with a sweet nutty flavor. The following is a really simple dish. Choose medium-size parsnips, not huge roots. Scrape or scrub clean.

Heat oven to 375 degrees

2 cups chopped or shredded parsnip
1-2 Tablespoons brown rice syrup or agave
1/2 teaspoon grated fresh ginger root or 1 teaspoon ginger powder

Mix all ingredients, lightly oil 4 X 7 baking dish and press mixture into baking dish. Bake for about 20 minutes.

Serves 8

◇◇◇

Waverly Root, in his encyclopedia, Foods, laments the unfortunate career of the parsnip, and regards it as "an unjustly neglected vegetable." Very popular in the Middle Ages, "it lost a formerly proud position in the domain of food through competition with the potato---an unlikely competitor, since it does not resemble the parsnip either in taste or texture." It is time to re-discover this wonderful vegetable for itself---no comparisons needed.

< 43 >

<< BROWN RICE CASSEROLE WITH PIGNOLI NUTS >>

Makes an excellent accompaniment to vegetable loaves, and can be served hot or warm.

Preheat oven to 350 degrees
Lightly oil an 8 X 10 inch baking dish.

1 Tablespoon olive oil
1 medium chopped onion
1 red or yellow pepper,
          cut into 1/2 inch squares
1 large carrot, cut in 1 inch pieces
2 large ribs of celery, cut in 1 inch pieces
3 cloves garlic, minced
2 bay leaves
1/2 teaspoon thyme
1 teaspoon dried dill weed
1/2 cup chopped fresh parsley, divided
1-1/2 teaspoons paprika
pinch of salt
1 cup uncooked long-grain brown rice
1-1/2 cups diced fresh tomatoes (or canned in winter)
1 cup water
1/4 cup raisins
1/2 cup toasted pignoli nuts

Heat oil in large skillet over medium heat. Add vegetables, garlic, bay leaves, thyme, dill, and 1/4 cup parsley. Cook over medium heat about 5-6 minutes. Stir often. Add paprika and rice. Continue cooking and stirring for 1 minute. Add tomatoes, water and raisins. Bring to a simmer. Remove bay leaves before serving.

Transfer to oiled baking dish. Cover and bake about 1-1/2 hours or until rice is tender. Toss with pignoli nuts and the remainder of the parsley.

Serves 6 generous portions
Tip: pignoli nuts are expensive. Try Trader Joe's, Costco, or the Internet.

< 44 >

What dish could be more traditional for the American harvest holiday than this one, yet it is based on a recipe from Bukharia, where stuffed pumpkin is a favorite dish. It was developed in a recipe in Gil Marks' book, Olive Trees and Honey: A Treasury of Vegetarian Recipes from Jewish Communities Around The World, which illustrates how foods often regarded as traditional to one culture can be found in other cultures as a traditional food there too.

Preheat oven to 375 degrees.

One 5 pound baking pumpkin, or kabocha squash
1 teaspoon sugar
pinch of salt

Make a lid for the pumpkin, by cutting off the top at a point where the pumpkin is about 4 inches in diameter. Scoop out seeds and loose fibers from the inside. Sprinkle with salt and sugar.

THE STUFFING

3 Tablespoons olive oil
1 large chopped onion
1-1/4 cups long grain brown rice
2 cups vegetable stock
1 scant teaspoon table salt
Ground black pepper
Pinch of saffron or 1/4 teaspoon turmeric
1 Tablespoon hot water
1/4 cup raisins
1/4 cup chopped parsley
1/2 cups cooked chickpeas
1 tart apple, peeled, chopped coarsely
one large cabbage leaf

Continue

< 45 >

Heat the oil over medium heat in a heavy saucepan. Add the onion and cook five minutes or until translucent. Mix in rice, stir to coat with oil, cook about 3 minutes. Add stock, salt and pepper, bring to a boil, cover, reduce heat to low and simmer until the liquid is absorbed, about 15 minutes---though the rice will be slightly undercooked.

Dissolve saffron in hot water, stir into the rice.

Add the rest of the ingredients, except for the cabbage leaf.

Pack the stuffing into the pumpkin, and replace the lid.

Line baking pan with parchment paper. Gil Marks recommends placing a large cabbage leaf under the pumpkin, to prevent the bottom of the pumpkin from burning. Add about 1 inch of water to pan. Bake for about 2 hours until pumpkin is tender.

You can serve just the filling by scooping it out, or serve the filling with a wedge of pumpkin, which makes a nice presentation.

Serves 8

Tip: If your oven is filled with other foods, the pumpkin can be cooked in a pot on the stove. Place it in a large pot with water up to an inch of the bottom of the pumpkin and bring the water to a boil. Cover, reduce the heat and simmer until pumpkin is tender.

< 46 >

<< SYRIAN PUMPKIN PATTIES >>

The pumpkin, again regarded as so traditionally American, has a thriving life in other cuisines. This dish, like the stuffed pumpkin, is also inspired by Gil Marks' book, *Olive Trees and Honey.*

Have ready cooked pumpkin. A 16 ounce can of pumpkin can be used.

1 cup fine bulgur

2 cups warm water or vegetable stock

2 cups mashed cooked pumpkin (about 2-1/2 pounds raw)

or use a 16 ounce can of pureéd pumpkin

(do not use canned pumpkin pie mix)

1 cup unbleached all-purpose flour

1/2 cup cold water

1 medium-size chopped onion

3 - 4 cloves minced garlic

1/2 teaspoon table salt

1/2 teaspoon ground coriander

1/2 teaspoon ground black pepper

1/4 teaspoon ground allspice

1/4 teaspoon ground cumin

Pinch of cayenne pepper

olive oil for frying

Soak bulgur in water or stock in a medium bowl for about 30 minutes. Drain.
Transfer bulgur to a food processor. Add the remaining ingredients, except the oil, and mix until well blended and smooth. If mixture seems thin, add a little more flour.

Shape mixture into oval patties about 1/2 inch thick, with hands coated with flour.

Heat the oil in a large skillet, fry patties until golden brown, turn once, about 2 minutes per side.

Can be served warm or at room temperature.

Makes about twelve patties.

< 47 >

<< TSIMMES >>

The word "tsimmes" means "all mixed up." It is a traditional Jewish dish and can be made in a variety of ways, with a variety of ingredients. Great for company because the dish is usually very large. Here are the most common ingredients, but you might find other ingredients you prefer.

3 medium-size white potatoes, scrubbed and quartered
3 large sweet potatoes, scrubbed and quartered
3 large carrots, scrubbed and cut into large chunks
2 Tablespoons of rice syrup or agave sauce
1 teaspoon cinnamon
1/2 teaspoon salt
1 cup of raisins

Place in a large pot, cover, and simmer slowly until the vegetables are tender.

Serves 8-10

Tip: Pumpkin and/or 2 tart apples can be added. But add apples 20 minutes before the dish is done, or you will get apple sauce mixed into the vegetables.

Add sautéed or browned tofu cubes to give dish a heartier feeling and/or to serve as an entrée.

Tip. To increase flavor of tofu in any tofu dish, press out water from tofu, cut into slices, cubes or triangles, and marinate in equal parts tamari sauce and red wine, with a small amount of olive oil. Marinated tofu will keep for a few days in refrigerator. Then sauté or use as indicated in any recipe.

< 48 >

Leeks have a fantastic flavor, even if you don't do anything to them, but this recipe, based on Gil Marks' book, *Olive trees and Honey,* is so exotic, finished with a lemon dressing, it's a great accompaniment to any entrée and, Marks suggests, it can even be served as an entrée itself.

Leeks have to be carefully washed, because grit gets trapped between the coiled leaves. The best way to do this is to pull the leaves gently apart, but do not separate, and flush out the sand and grit with swiftly running water from the faucet. You will quickly get the hang of it.

Leeks were considered so tempting by the Hebrews who fled slavery, that they even considered returning to Egypt and to slavery (or so the story goes) in order to return to the leeks they loved so well.

2-1/2 cups of water
5-6 cloves of garlic, crushed
strips of lemon peel from one lemon
2 bay leaves
1 cinnamon stick (about 2 inches)
pinch of fresh grated nutmeg
2 pounds of leeks (about 10) white and light green parts only
(some people prefer to cut away the dark green ends)

Put water in a large pot or roasting pan and bring water to a low boil. Add the garlic, lemon zest, bay leaves, cinnamon stick and nutmeg. Simmer about 10 minutes. Add leeks in a single layer, cover, simmer for 15 minutes. Drain (reserve liquid for soup). Transfer leeks to a serving platter.

Continue

< 49 >

6 Tablespoons fresh lemon juice
1 teaspoon sea salt
1/4 teaspoon cayenne pepper
1/4 teaspoon ground white or black pepper
pinch of saffron or 1/4 teaspoon ground turmeric
1 Tablespoon vegetable oil

For the dressing, combine the first five ingredients in a bowl. Whisk in the oil in a slow stream. Drizzle this over the leeks and refrigerate over night.

Servings: 8-10

Tip: This dressing will also work well with grilled or lightly sautéed asparagus. Figure about 4 asparagus stalks per serving (Cut or snap off bottom quarter of each stalk.)

◇

Leeks are one of the most ancient foods, and will grow well even in cold climates. They are the national emblem of Wales, and Welshmen wear bits of leek on St. David's Day to commemorate the victory of King Cadwallader over the Saxons in 640 CE. Yet, in spite of the fact that leeks like a cold climate, their association with the Bible makes people think of leeks as a warm climate vegetable. It is true that the Egyptians cultivated leeks at the dawn of their history, but wild leeks grow freely all over Wales.

< 50 >

This recipe comes from a cookbook collection made by members of the North Shore CSA (Community Supported Agriculture) in Massachusetts. In those early days of establishing CSA's, many of us collected recipes based on the great produce we received, and often had cookouts and picnics together.

1 Tablespoon plus 1 teaspoon olive oil
2 large onions, chopped
4 cloves garlic, minced
2-1/4 cups arborio rice (best kind for this risotto)
5-3/4 cups vegetarian broth
3/4 cups dry white wine
1 teaspoon dried thyme or 1 Tablespoon fresh thyme
3 Tablespoons fresh chives, chopped
2 cups torn arugula
Freshly round pepper
Salt to taste
1/2 pound sliced mushrooms
1/2 cup grated vegan Parmesan cheese or
nutritional yeast

Heat 1 Tablespoon olive oil in a large pot, sauté the onion and garlic for 5 minutes.

Stir in rice and sauté another 5 minutes until rice browns slightly.
Pour in half the broth, all of the wine, herbs, salt and pepper.

Bring to a boil, stir, lower heat and simmer, cover. Cook for 30-45 minutes. Stir vigorously every 10-15 minutes. Add remaining broth after the first 15 minutes.

When most of the liquid is absorbed, lightly sauté mushrooms and arugula in a skillet with remaining teaspoon of oil. When rice has absorbed most of the liquid in the big pot, add mushrooms and arugula to it. Stir well.

Serves 6-8

< 51 >

Inspired by a recipe from Dara Goldstein's *The Vegetarian Hearth*, this casserole is just the thing for an autumn dinner.

Preheat oven to 375 degrees. Lightly grease a 2-quart casserole.

3 large potatoes
2 Tablespoons Earth Balance® spread--or the equivalent
1 medium-size onion, chopped fine
2 Tablespoons tomato paste
2 teaspoons curry powder
5 Tablespoons unbleached all purpose flour
1 cup almond or coconut milk
1 cup water
1 teaspoon salt
Fresh ground pepper

Boil unpeeled potatoes in slightly salted water in covered pot until just tender, about 35 minutes.

Drain, and cool slightly. Peel or not--it's up to you. Cut into cubes. You should have about 5 cups of potato cubes.

Melt Earth Balance® in large saucepan, sauté chopped onion for about ten minute, until golden. Add the tomato paste, curry powder, and flour. Mix well. Stir in the milk and water. Add salt and pepper to taste. Bring to a boil and simmer for 3 minutes.

Put the mixture into the greased casserole and bake for 30 minutes.

Serves 6

Tip: Can be increased to serve more by adding one or more potatoes. But be sure to increase tomato paste and adjust seasonings by 25% to 50% more. May take some experimenting.

< 52 >

Based on a Jewish recipe for cholent, a great variation on the ratatouville with a spicy Middle Eastern flavor, inspired by Gabi Shahar. You can vary the spices. Start this dish twenty-four hours before serving because, like traditional cholents, it cooks in the oven for at least ten hours. Good for large crowds.

3 Tablespoons olive oil
2 medium-size onions chopped
2 cloves of garlic, chopped
1 inch of fresh ginger grated, or 1 teaspoon of ground commercial ginger
4 Tablespoons of curry powder
1 large can crushed tomatoes. Keep juice
1 cup vegan sour cream
6 potatoes, scrubbed and cut in chunks (peeling is opional)
2 yams or sweet potatoes, scrubbed and cut in chunks
2 carrots, scrubbed, cut into chunks
1/2 pound of dried beans (your choice)
Salt and pepper to taste

Heat oven to 220 degrees

Two hours ahead of cooking, cover beans with water in a pot, bring to a boil. Boil 3 minutes, remove from fire, let beans rest for 2 hours. Drain and rinse.

Heat oil in a large oven-poof pot with tight-fitting lid. Sauté chopped onions, garlic and ginger over low flame, 10-15 minutes. Add curry, and sauté another 2 minutes. Add tomatoes, with juice from the can, cover, cook ten minutes, stir occasionally.

Add potatoes, yams, carrots and beans. Cover with boiling water 1/2 inch over the top. Cover with a fitting lid, and place in oven for about ten hours.

Before serving, add vegan sour cream, salt and pepper to taste. Mix well.

Serves 12

< 53 >

Portobellos are marvelously succulent mushrooms and can make any dish hearty. If you desire, add a few of the more expensive mushrooms, like shiitake and porcini. A few of these go a long way to make this dish very rich. Excellent for an intimate holiday meal.

1 cup of yellow cornmeal, medium grind
(or use Bob's Red Mill polenta. Pre-made polenta can also be used.)
4 cups of boiling water
2 teaspoons salt
2 Tablespoons Earth Balance® or equivalent
1/2 cup vegan Parmesan cheese or nutritional yeast
1 small can of corn kernels, mixed into the cooked polenta

Cook cornmeal in the top of double boiler, pour in the boiling water, stir until well mixed. Add the salt. Fit top of the boiler into the bottom, filled with 2 inches of boiling water, cover and steam the polenta for 30-45 minutes. Stir occasionally. When the polenta is thickened, add Earth Balance® and vegan cheese (or nutritional yeast).

For Topping
1 small onion, chopped fine
2 cloves garlic, minced
3 Tablespoons olive oil
1-1/2 pounds sliced portobellos, mixed with
1/4-1/2 pound of wild or other mushrooms
1/2 teaspoon salt
Freshly ground black pepper
1 Tablespoon dried oregano
3 Tablespoons of Italian parsley

Sauté onions and garlic in the olive oil in a skillet, add the mushrooms, sauté 5-8 minutes, turn once to brown both sides. Lower heat, add seasoning and herbs, mix well, cook another 5-7 minutes. Top the polenta with mushroom mixture. Serve with a green salad.

Serves 4-5

< 54 >

<<BAKED SAUERKRAUT WITH APPLES>>

A unique hot relish that offers the palette a tart accompaniment to a meal. It takes some time to cook, but very little work

Preheat oven to 325 degrees

2 Tablespoons of Earth Balance® or the equivalent
1 onion, sliced
28 ounces of sauerkraut, drained
3 medium apples, peeled and diced--not too fine.
(Do not use Delicious apples. For a tarter taste, use granny smith apples)
1-1/2 cups white wine
1/2 cup vegetable stock
1 teaspoon brown sugar
1 teaspoon celery seed

Heat Earth Balance® (or equivalent) in oven in a large, oven proof casserole dish that has a cover. Add onions and saute´ until transparent.

Add sauerkraut, mix well, cook uncovered over low heat for 5 minutes.

Add apples, wine and enough stock to cover. Mix well, and cook for 30 minutes.

Stir in sugar and celery seeds, cover, transfer to oven. Taste, adjusting for sugar. Bake 30 minutes.

Serve hot.

Serves 6-8 as a hot relish

< 55 >

Sweet potatoes are such a traditional favorite for harvest holidays, and there are many ways to make a sweet potato casserole or pudding. Use your favorite, if you have one, or try the one below for something different. The next three recipes were included in a cookbook compiled by the CSA on the North Shore in Massachusetts in its early days.

Preheat oven to 350 degrees

3 cups of sweet potatoes
1/2 mashed banana or egg replacer for 2 eggs
1 teaspoon of vanilla
1/4 cup sugar
1/2 cup almond or soy milk
1/4 cup or 1/2 stick Earth Balance® or equivalent

Bake 3 large sweet potatoes until soft. Cool, scoop out the potatoes.

Add the rest of the ingredients, mix well and place in a baking dish.

TOPPING
1/2 cup unbleached flour
1/2 cup brown sugar
1/2 cup chopped cashews or almonds
1/2 cup Earth Balance®

Mix ingredients and crumble on top of the casserole.

Bake for 30 minutes

Serves 6

< 56 >

Another great sweet potato casserole. This one should be prepared a day or two in advance, since its flavors improve overnight.

4 large sweet potatoes, washed and peeled
4 medium baking apples, washed, cored, but not peeled
3/4 cup applesauce
1 teaspoon cinnamon

Slice and layer potatoes and apples to fill at least a 2 quart casserole.

Layer in the ingredients, starting with the potatoes, then the apples. Sprinkle seasoning over the top. End with a layer of applesauce.

Cover casserole. Bake about an hour until potatoes and apples are soft.

Serves 8-10

Tip: For sweet potatoes, use red garnet yams---they're more expensive, but worth it for a holiday.

Use firm apples, such as Cortlands that hold their shape during baking.

< 57 >

Here is an unusual use of the sweet potato, based on an original recipe submitted by a member of the North Shore CSA. It's flexible, you can omit the pinto beans, and use a Tablespoon of cajun flavoring instead of the chili. You can even throw in a handful of dried cranberries for looks and taste. But make early or the day before, so the flavors can mix.

2 Tablespoons olive oil
1 large onion
2 cloves garlic, minced
3-4 Tablespoons chili powder
1 cup vegetable broth
2-3 large sweet potatoes, peeled and cubed
2 14-1/2 ounce cans of diced tomatoes
1 small can pinto beans (optional)
1 small can black beans
1 ten ounce package frozen corn
3 Tablespoons chopped cilantro (optional)
3 teaspoons grated orange peel,
or a 1 teaspoon of orange flavoring

Heat oil in skillet over high heat.
Add onion and minced garlic, sauté until lightly browned.

Add chili powder or cajun spice mix, stir for a minute. Add broth and potatoes. Cook for about 15 minutes until potato chunks begin to soften. Cover skillet, reduce heat to medium.

Add tomatoes (with juice) add beans, corn, and cilantro, if using.
Simmer uncovered for another 15 minutes, or until chili thickens
Sprinkle grated orange or flavoring into mixture.

Serves 6 easily as a side dish.

Tip: If you want to use cilantro and find it too strong, mix it half and half with minced parsley.
Leftover use for next day, mix in sautéed veggie pups and heat mixture altogether.

< 58 >

FOR THE SWEET PALATE

SWEET BREADS AND DESSERTS

< 59 >

This is an easy recipe. If you are making many dishes and don't want to work too hard on dessert, or you are taking a dish to a holiday event and want something easy, but with much taste and visual appeal, try this.

Make a graham cracker crust, using the directions on the box. If it calls for butter, use Earth Balance® or grape seed oil. Add a teaspoon of vanilla to the ingredients. A glass pie pan works well for this. Or you can buy a pre-made crust.

Why do we call this a cheesecake, when it contains no cheese? Actually it does, tofu is soy cheese. (Yes, cheese can be made from beans or nuts as well as dairy).

Preheat oven to 325 degrees.

1 graham cracker crust – store bought or homemade (use 8 or 9-inch pie pan)

I pound of firm tofu
¾ cup maple syrup
2 Tablespoons grape seed oil
1 Tablespoon lemon juice
pinch of salt

Press some water out of the tofu. Put all ingredients in a blender or food processor and work up to high speed. Blend until very creamy.

Pour the mixture over the crust, being careful not to get any on the edges. Smooth the top. Bake for 20-25 minutes. When the middle does not look soft, it has set. Remove from the oven, cool to room temperature, then chill in refrigerator. Top with berries, fresh in warm climates, or frozen in winter for added appeal.

There is something about cheesecake that most people enjoy. The contrast of the creamy filling and the slightly crunchy crust is a winning combination. Although this book features harvest holiday recipes, remember this one when berries are at their best.

Serves 6-8

< 60 >

<<CHOCOLATE TOFU PIE>>

Inspired by the wonderful book, *Tofu Cookery* by Louise Hagler. Once you get the hang of it, you can improvise all kinds of variations on this theme. We haven't met anyone who doesn't like this pie.

Preheat oven to 350 degrees.

Graham Cracker Crust
1-1/2 cups graham cracker crumbs
1/4 cup (or 1/2 stick) margarine, cut in small pieces

Grind graham crackers thoroughly in a food processor. Add margarine and continue processing until crumbs are well combined with it. Press mixture in the bottom and sides of a 9-inch pie pan.

Filling
1 cup semi-sweet chocolate chips
2 Tablespoons water
1 pound soft or silken tofu
1/4 cup soy milk
1/3 cup agave syrup
1 teaspoon vanilla extract

In a heavy bottomed sauce pan, or the top of a double boiler, melt the chocolate chips with 2 Tablespoons of water.
Clean bowl of processor thoroughly, and put tofu with the melted chocolate into the processor and process until smooth. Stir in remaining ingredients.

Pour filling into the crust, bake 30-35 minutes, until filling is firm and crust is golden.

Can be made a day ahead. May be served at room temperature or chilled.

Serves 6-8

< 61 >

Always desirable, this classic chocolate cake is moist and rich and can be embellished with walnuts, raspberries, or both. How rich do you want this?

Preheat oven to 350 degrees.

1 cup sugar
1-1/2 cups flour
1/2 teaspoon salt
1/4 cup cocoa
1 teaspoon baking soda
1 Tablespoon vinegar
1/3 cup vegetable oil
1 teaspoon vanilla flavoring
1 cup cold water

Sift first five ingredients into an ungreased 8 X 8 baking pan. Add remaining ingredients and stir gently until smooth. Bake 35 minutes. And there you have it! Can anything be easier?

Serves 8

In fact, it is so easy, that you can easily make two by doubling ingredients and bake in a 9 X 13 pan. This can then be split in half and used as layers--or make two of the 8 X 8 size and use these as layers. Spread crushed raspberries between the layers, top with more crushed raspberries and chopped walnut, or with tofu cream, store bought or made by you.

Will serve about 15

Tip: Do not crush the raspberries to the point where you lose the delineation of the fruit and it turns into jam. The raspberries and the walnuts should be distinct.

Variations: The smaller cake can also be split, filled with slightly softened tofu ice cream and covered with a fudgy chocolate ice cream. Or the icing can be the filler, and the ice cream can be used to serve it a la mode.

< 62 >

This is more cake-like than pudding---denser and a bit crumbly, but offers richness to your holiday dinner. A little goes a long way.

Preheat oven to 350 degrees.

12 Tablespoons Earth Balance ® softened

3/4 cup brown sugar

1/4 cup liquid vegan coffee creamer

1-1/2 cups whole-wheat pastry flour or white whole wheat flour

½ teaspoon sea salt

1- ½ teaspoons baking powder

1 -1/2 cups grated carrot (about 3 large carrots)

Juice of half a lemon

1 teaspoon baking soda (dissolve in 2 Tablespoons hot water)

Lightly oil an 8-inch square pan.
Grate the carrots by hand, or use the food processor. By hand, mix the margarine, brown sugar and creamer until well mixed in.
In another bowl combine flour, salt and baking powder, stir well.
Add the flour mixture, carrots and lemon juice to the margarine mixture.
When well mixed, add the baking soda mixture and stir in well.
Spread in the pan, bake for 30 to 35 minutes.
For a glass pan, you can reduce the heat by 25 degrees.

White whole- wheat flour is similar to whole- wheat pastry flour.
For a gluten-free version substitute Bob's Red Mill All-Purpose Baking Mix,® with a teaspoon of added xanthan gum, which is a thickener.

SERVES 12-14

Tip: a dollop of soy ice cream goes nicely on the top

< 63 >

<< BANANA CAKE >>

Will add variety to your holiday dessert selection. When bananas get too soft to eat, peel and freeze and use in baking.

2 cups whole-wheat pastry flour or white whole-wheat flour
1 teaspoon baking soda
2 teaspoons non-aluminum baking powder
¼ teaspoon sea salt
2 teaspoons cinnamon
1 teaspoon ginger
½ teaspoon each nutmeg and cloves
1 cup organic sugar
½ cup grape seed oil
2 teaspoons vanilla
4 small bananas or 3 large
½ cup soy milk with 1 teaspoon apple cider vinegar added
a cup of raisins or walnuts or 1/2 half cup of both (optional)

Preheat oven to 350 degrees.

First add the vinegar to the soy milk to make "buttermilk" for a tender texture.

Sift the flour with the salt, baking powder, soda and spices. (A strainer makes a good sifter.)

Add raisins/nuts if using and coat well with the flour.

In a small bowl, mash the bananas with a fork. Add the wet ingredients and the bananas alternately to the flour mixture. Go easy. Over mixing causes dryness.

Lightly oil a 9x13 pan. Bake at 350 degrees for 30 -35 minutes or until a toothpick comes out clean.

TIP: A light frosting adds appeal. To make, mix about 2 Tablespoons Earth Balance® margarine with a cup of sifted powdered sugar, two teaspoons sherry or lemon juice and a teaspoon vanilla. Mixture should be soft but not too runny. Drizzle or spread it on in bits.

SERVES about 12

< 64 >

<< SKILLET CORNBREAD >>

A mutual friend, Alexandra Santilli, made this for us. She had adapted it from an old vegetarian cookbook from the 1970's. So for this recipe, haul out that cast iron skillet that you don't use but still have.

This cornbread is versatile. You can serve it with the meal, as another dessert, or with brunch the next day.

Preheat oven to 400 degrees.

1-1/2 cups fine or medium grain cornmeal
1-1/2 cups whole-wheat pastry flour
1 Tablespoon non-aluminum baking powder
1 teaspoon baking soda
1 Tablespoon sugar
1 teaspoon sea salt
2 -½ cups soy milk with 2 teaspoons apple cider vinegar added
¼ cup grape seed oil

Lightly oil a 10-inch cast iron skillet and place in the oven to heat. Mix the dry ingredients well, stir in the milk and oil. Pour into the hot skillet and bake 30 minutes on the top rack of oven. If you are careful, you may brown the top under the broiler for a very few minutes. Pay close attention.

A nice addition – 2 cups corn kernels, canned, thawed frozen or fresh local, if in season.
A more savory version: add 1 small onion chopped and lightly sautéed first and/or 1 can of diced green chilis.

SERVING: Eight generous wedges or about a dozen smaller ones.

< 65 >

Can we imagine Harvest Holidays without something pumpkin? Never. These pumpkin muffins, adapted from Isa Chandra Moskowitz's book, are a change from pie and can also be served as dessert, or with the meal instead of bread. These muffins are made with whole wheat pastry flour and have less sugar, but still have a great flavor and texture.

Preheat oven to 400 degrees.

1- ¾ cup sifted whole-wheat pastry flour or whole-wheat white flour
(available from King Arthur)
1 Tablespoon non-aluminum baking powder
1/4 teaspoon sea salt
1/4 teaspoon cinnamon
1/2 teaspoon each ginger and nutmeg
1/4 teaspoon allspice
1/8 teaspoon cloves
I cup organic sugar
1 cup puréed pumpkin (use fresh pumpkin or canned organic pumpkin if it is available) Do not use pumpkin pie mix. The seasonings will clash with our seasonings.
½ cup soy milk with 1 teaspoon apple cider vinegar added
1/2 cup grape seed oil
2 Tablespoons molasses
1 cup walnuts or dried cranberries, or 1/2 cup each (optional)

Sift together flour, sugar, baking powder, salt and spices. In a large, separate bowl mix the wet ingredients. Pour the wet into the dry, mix gently until just well combined.

Line a 12 cup muffin tin with paper (not foil) baking cups. Or use a mini-muffin pan, makes 24.

Fill muffin cups 3/4 full. Bake 18-20 minutes. A toothpick should come out clean.

TIP: A dollop of apricot jam on the top turns this into a sweet dessert.

< 66 >

<<APPLE PIE>>

Old-fashioned, but always popular. Every one has an apple pie recipe, but this one is different enough to include.

Preheat oven to 425 degrees.

Step one

> 1 cup unbleached white flour
> 2 cups whole wheat pastry flour
> 1/4 cup organic sugar (optional)
> 1/8 teaspoon baking powder

Combine these ingredients in the food processor, or mix with electric mixer or by hand.

Step two

> Spray of grape seed oil
> 1 cup Earth Balance®
> 1/2 cup ice water

Brush or spray a 9-inch pie plate with oil. Cut margarine into dry ingredients until it resembles grains of sand. Slowly stir in half the ice water with a fork and continue stirring until dough starts to come together. Add the rest of the water a little at a time if the dough is too dry and crumbly. Gather the dough into a ball, form into a disk and wrap in plastic wrap. Refrigerate for at least 30 minutes.

Step three

> 8 to 10 large Golden Delicious apples,
>   peeled, cored and sliced
> 2 teaspoons cinnamon
> 1 Tablespoon lemon juice
> 1/2 cup maple syrup
> 1/2 cup arrowroot flour
> 1 teaspoon vanilla

Mix together all of the above ingredients until thoroughly combined. Roll out dough into circle about 12 inches. Transfer to pie pan and prick bottom. Pile with the apple mixture and roll out top crust. Place top crust over apples.

(Continue)

< 67 >

Press edges of crust together

Flute any way you wish and prick in several places. Place dough on bottom rack at 425° for 10 minutes. Then lower oven temperature to 375° and bake until crust is lightly browned and the filling is bubbling, about 40 to 50 minutes.

Cool at least 1 hour before serving.

Serves 8 to 10 slices.

TIP: Not sweet enough? Pass the vegan ice cream to top this off.

The apple has been called the "king of fruits." It is certainly one of the most versatile of fruits, and possibly one of the oldest-- and it is responsible for starting the scientific revolution. Everyone knows the story of how a falling apple led Isaac Newton to the laws of gravity. Most people think this is a legend---but check Wikipedia.

Books have been written about the apple, and legends abound about it. According to the Bible, it was the apple which tempted Eve to disobey God. In Greek legend, it was the apple which Paris offered to Aphrodite when he had to choose between her, Juno and Minerva in the first beauty contest in history. He chose Aphrodite, and in return Aphrodite awarded Paris the beauty of Helen, who was the wife of Menelaus, king of Sparta All hell broke loose---known as the Trojan wars! Hence, the proverb that one rotten apple spoils the bunch.

< 68 >

Is this cake or bread? Make it and you decide.

Preheat oven 350 degrees.

> **Grape seed oil**
> **1 cup margarine**
> **1 1/2 cups maple syrup**
> **1/4 cup Mori Nu tofu, puréed (see glossary)**
> **1 1/2 cups non-dairy milk**
> **1 Tablespoon lemon zest, chopped fine**

Oil two 9" cake pans. Line with parchment paper if you have it and oil again, or oil pans and dust with flour. Whip above ingredients in an electric mixer, food processor or blender until well mixed, about 3 minutes.

> **3 cups unbleached white flour**
> **1 cup cornmeal**
> **2 Tablespoons baking powder**
> **1/2 teaspoon salt**

Sift these ingredients. Add to the wet ingredients above and combine well, being careful not to over-mix. Pour into pans, smooth batter and bake approximately 35 minutes or until the center springs back when touched and the sides are browned and pulling away from the side of the pan. Cool pans on cooling rack for 10 minutes, then invert onto rack and cool thoroughly before frosting.

Frosting
1 block semi-firm tofu, drained
1 container dairy free cream cheese

4 oz margarine
1/2 cup maple syrup

2 cups black raspberry jelly
1 teaspoon lemon rind

Continue

< 69 >

Blend everything but the jelly and lemon rind in the food processor until smooth and creamy, scraping down the bowl a few times. Chill one hour.

Invert the first layer on to a plate or turntable so that the bottom is on the top. Brush crumbs away from cake and cut first layer in half horizontally. Remove top carefully. Stir jelly to loosen for easier spreading. Apply a thin layer of jelly over the layer. Add the top and repeat. Repeat with the next layer, leaving the top plain. Apply a thick layer of the tofu frosting to the top. Spread jelly smoothly around the sides of the cake, leave plain. Sprinkle with the lemon rind or use thinly sliced lemons.

Servings: 8-10 slices

<< PUMPKIN ICE CREAM PIE >>

A good timesaver--and one that children can make---it's always nice to include them in the cooking---if possible.

2 quarts vegan vanilla ice cream (such as Soy Delicious® Vanilla bean)
1 cup organic canned pumpkin
2 teaspoons pumpkin pie spice
½ cup brown sugar packed
I graham cracker crust – buy it or make it

Soften the ice cream, mix with the pumpkin, seasonings, and brown sugar. Fill the pie crust. Cover and freeze for 1 hour.

Some slivers of crystallized ginger can be added on top for taste and eye appeal.

SERVES 6-8

< 70 >

<<SWEET POTATO PIE>>

This pie can be a dessert or a side dish---as you wish. Crust is easy to make, even if you have never made pie crust before--or you can buy a vegan pie crust.

CRUST FOR ONE 9-INCH CRUST
1 cup unbleached flour
½ cup whole-wheat pastry flour
¼ teaspoon sea salt
One stick Earth Balance ® vegan margarine (available in sticks)
2 Tablespoons ice water

For best results, chill everything, including the flour. Mix the flour and salt, then crumble in the Earth Balance. Use a pastry blender or two forks, if you don't have a pastry blender. Add the water slowly. The mixture will gradually form a ball. Then roll out on a floured board until it is a disc that is larger than the pie pan. Place gently in the pan, pat into the bottom and sides. Trim the edges, use leftover trimming to patch bare spots in crust. Pinch edges or use fork tines all around.

FILLING
Buy pumpkin pie spice, or make your own by mixing 4 Tablespoons cinnamon, 4 teaspoons each nutmeg and ginger and 3 teaspoons all-spice

2 large yams or orange sweet potatoes
¾ cup non-dairy milk
4 Tablespoons molasses
1 Tablespoon organic sugar
1 Tablespoon pumpkin pie spices
Ener G ® Egg Replacer equal to two eggs (directions are on the box)

Bake yams at 400 degrees for an hour (or cook in microwave for about seven minutes.) When cool, remove skin and mash, mix in non-dairy milk, spices and sweeteners. Mix egg replacer separately, then pour into the yam mixture. Bake for 10 minutes at 400 degrees, reduce temperature to 350, and bake another 40 to 50 minutes.

SERVES 8

< 71 >